PRACTICAL PROGRAM EVALUATION FOR CRIMINAL JUSTICE

PRACTICAL PROGRAM EVALUATION FOR CRIMINAL JUSTICE

GENNARO F. VITO
GEORGE E. HIGGINS

LONDON AND NEW YORK

First published 2015 by Anderson Publishing

Published 2015 by Routledge
2 Park Square, Milton Park, Abingdon, Oxon OX14 4RN

and by Routledge
711 Third Avenue, New York, NY 10017

Routledge is an imprint of the Taylor & Francis Group, an informa business

Copyright © 2015 Taylor & Francis. All rights reserved.

No part of this book may be reprinted or reproduced or utilised in any form or by any electronic, mechanical, or other means, now known or hereafter invented, including photocopying and recording, or in any information storage or retrieval system, without permission in writing from the publishers.

Notices
No responsibility is assumed by the publisher for any injury and/or damage to persons or property as a matter of products liability, negligence or otherwise, or from any use of operation of any methods, products, instructions or ideas contained in the material herein.

Practitioners and researchers must always rely on their own experience and knowledge in evaluating and using any information, methods, compounds, or experiments described herein. In using such information or methods they should be mindful of their own safety and the safety of others, including parties for whom they have a professional responsibility.

Product or corporate names may be trademarks or registered trademarks, and are used only for identification and explanation without intent to infringe.

This book and the individual contributions contained in it are protected under copyright by the Publisher (other than as may be noted herein).

Library of Congress Cataloging-in-Publication Data
Application Submitted

British Library Cataloguing-in-Publication Data
A catalogue record for this book is available from the British Library

ISBN-13: 978-1-4557-7770-9 (pbk)

Dedication

To the Vito and Higgins families.

CONTENTS

Digital Assets xi
Preface xiii

Chapter 1   Getting Started with Program Evaluation 1
Introduction 1
Administrator and Evaluator 2
Strengths and Weaknesses of Program Evaluation 3
Evidence-Based Practices 5
Meta-Analysis 9
Campbell Collaboration (Crime and Justice Group) 12
Summary 12
Discussion Questions 13
References 13

Chapter 2   Planning a Program Evaluation 15
Introduction 15
Problem-Oriented Policing 16
Planning an Evaluation Strategy 18
Logic Model 22
Politics of Evaluation Research 24
Ethical Issues in Evaluation Research 25
Summary 29
Discussion Questions 29
References 30

Chapter 3   Needs Assessment Evaluation 31
Introduction 31
Definition of Needs 32
Data Sources 34
Problems with Needs Assessment 43

Summary..44
Discussion Questions..................................44
References...44

Chapter 4   Theory-Driven Evaluation............................47
Introduction...47
Evaluability Assessment Approach......................49
Describing and Producing Program Theory...............50
Analyzing Program Theory..............................57
Summary..61
Discussion Questions..................................61
References...61
Additional Readings....................................62

Chapter 5   Process Evaluation...................................63
Introduction...63
Process Evaluation: Program Implementation............64
Process Evaluation: Monitoring Conduct of Evaluation
Research Design..66
Process Evaluation: Use of Qualitative Methods........69
Process Evaluation Assessment: Evidence-Based
Correctional Program Checklist........................75
Summary..76
Discussion Questions..................................77
References...77

Chapter 6   Outcome Evaluation...................................79
Introduction...80
Classic Experimental Design...........................80
To Experiment or not to Experiment?...................85
Quasi-Experimental Research Design....................87
Before-and-After Design (One Group Pre-Test, Post-Test Design)....91
Question of Causation.................................93

Summary...94
Discussion Questions.................................94
References...94

Chapter 7 Cost-efficiency Evaluation 97
Introduction...97
Costs..99
Limits of Cost Analyses.............................108
Summary..109
Discussion Questions................................109
References..110

Chapter 8 Measurement and Data Analysis..............111
Introduction..111
Measurement...112
Statistics..117
Summary..126
Discussion Questions................................126
References..126

Chapter 9 Reporting and Using Evaluations............127
Introduction..127
Review of Operation CeaseFire Chicago 128
Factors Influencing the Use of Program Evaluation Results........136
Summary..139
Discussion Questions................................139
References..140

Chapter 10 Looking Ahead: A Call to Action in Evaluation Research 141
Introduction..142
Point 1: Use the Best Possible Research Design 142
Point 2: Evaluators must get Involved in the Very
Beginning of the Program 142

Point 3: Evaluators must Include Some Measure of Cost in their Analyses 143
Point 4: Evaluation Leads to the Development of Evidence-Based Practice 144
Point 5: Get out into the Field 144
Point 6: Prepare to Partner with Practitioners 145
Conclusion. 146
Discussion Questions. 146
References. 147

Glossary. 149
Index 157

DIGITAL ASSETS

Interactive resources can be accessed for free by registering at www.routledge.com/cw/vito

For the Instructor

- *Test bank:* Compose, customize, and deliver exams using an online assessment package in a free Windows-based authoring tool that makes it easy to build tests using the unique multiple-choice and true or false questions created for *Practical Program Evaluation for Criminal Justice*. What's more, this authoring tool allows you to export customized exams directly to Blackboard, WebCT, eCollege, Angel, and other leading systems. All test bank files are also conveniently offered in Word format.
- *PowerPoint lecture slides:* Reinforce key topics with focused PowerPoint slides that provide a perfect visual outline with which to augment your lecture. Each individual book chapter has its own dedicated slideshow.
- *Instructor's guides:* Design your course around customized learning objectives, discussion questions, and other instructor tools.

PREFACE

Job training in prison, rehabilitation programming, or policing tactics are all organized ways that individuals or organizations attempt to achieve their goals in criminal justice. A substantial amount of resources and effort result in a number of services and products that help those involved with criminal justice to meet the needs of society. The criminal justice system includes programs, facilities, and policies to help individuals lead fruitful, satisfying, healthier, or safer lives. Primarily, those involved with the criminal justice system have needs that are being met through publicly funded efforts. These efforts are called programs. The methods that are used to plan, monitor, or improve programming are the basis of program evaluation. The evaluation methods in this book apply not only to criminal justice, but to public and private agencies and for-profit organizations.

Management is a component of the success of a criminal justice program. Attempts to improve productivity or employee morale all require good planning techniques, feedback on the impact of the plan, and the utilization of the feedback. This book and the examples within reflect publicly funded programming, and the principles of program evaluation have been widely used in criminal justice.

The book is arranged in a manner reflecting all of the pieces of an evaluation. Chapter 1 provides the basic definitions of the book. Chapter 2 provides the basics of planning a program evaluation, and the issues that an evaluator needs to be aware of when conducting an evaluation. Chapter 3 provides the foundation of a needs evaluation. The book then shifts into developing an understanding of the underlying theory of the program. Chapter 4 is focused on theory evaluation. Chapter 5 moves the reader through the different parts of a process evaluation. Chapter 6 focuses on an outcomes and impact evaluation. Chapter 7 helps the reader understand the issues involved in a cost-efficiency evaluation. In Chapter 8 the reader gets some perspective on how measurement and statistics are used in program evaluations. Chapter 9 provides the reader with an overview of writing a report and the uses of an evaluation. Chapter 10 provides a call to action in criminal justice program evaluation.

We wrote this book in the hope that improved evaluation will lead to more effective and efficient programming in criminal justice. We give all students this charge.

Gennaro F. Vito and George E. Higgins
University of Louisville

GETTING STARTED WITH PROGRAM EVALUATION

Keywords

systematic review
Maryland Report
meta-analysis
Campbell Collaboration (Crime and Justice Group)

CHAPTER OUTLINE
Introduction 1
Administrator and Evaluator 2
Strengths and Weaknesses of Program Evaluation 3
Evidence-Based Practices 5
   Maryland Report   6
      "What Works"   6
      "What's Promising"   7
      "What Doesn't Work"   8
Meta-Analysis 9
Campbell Collaboration (Crime and Justice Group) 12
Summary 12
Discussion Questions 13
References 13

Program evaluation is the systematic assessment of the operation and/or outcomes of a program or policy, compared to a set of implicit or explicit standards, as a means of contributing to the improvement of the program or policy.

—Carol Weiss (1998)

Introduction

The aim of program evaluation is to determine the effectiveness of an intervention. In this book, we are interested in the effectiveness of crime prevention programs, whether they are aimed at individuals (treatment of offenders or victims, prosecution of career criminals) or communities (crime prevention programs), and the operations of the components of the criminal justice system (police, courts, corrections—both juvenile and adult).

The measurement of efficiency is the key problem faced by an evaluation researcher. Accountability can only be established if the evaluation measures are valid indicators of performance. Of course, the measures must also be readily available. Evaluation of crime programs is a significant exercise that can have a direct impact on society. Effective crime programs are vitally needed to deal with the crime problem and all the facets of public safety, such as rising crime rates, fear of crime among the public, crowded jails and prisons, and government expenditures. The pressure for information to deal with these issues is evident. The role of evaluation research in criminal justice is to provide evidence about the effects of programs and policies that are designed to enhance public safety in a manner that is accessible and informative to policy makers (Lipsey, 2005, p. 8). This text will provide an introduction to the research methods and guidelines necessary to conduct a successful evaluation.

Administrator and Evaluator

As Adams (1975, p. 5) has indicated, there are two significant actors in the evaluation process: the program administrator and the evaluator. The *administrator* must be committed to research and the creation of an organizational climate that encourages the production, reporting, and use of the findings of the evaluation. The *evaluator* must guide the conduct of the research process from beginning to end: its structure and methodology, use of valid measures of performance, and maintaining the balance between theory and practical, applied policy implications of the results. These two actors must work together and communicate well to produce a valid and reliable program evaluation. Each has different sources of expertise: the administrator knows what the program was designed to do and how it should operate, and the evaluator has methodological skills and knows how to design accurate research projects.

Suchman (1974, p. 5) identified three major aspects of the demand for evaluation research:

- The social problem (in our case, crime).
- The service agencies (the components of the criminal justice system).
- The public (who seek protection from crime).

Again, the emphasis is on the determination of the worth of programs and policies designed to prevent crime. Of course, this is why the term *evaluation* is so pertinent. In this text, we will be concerned with the determination of the research methods and techniques that can accurately assess the value of a crime program.

Monitoring is necessary to establish accountability for program results. Program evaluation informs the monitoring process. Traditionally, such monitoring assumes two forms: external and internal. Public agencies, like those in the criminal justice system, are externally accountable to political authorities and must regularly report to them about activities and processes. Internally, criminal justice agencies must provide useful, decision-oriented information on the program compliance of their facilities to flag problems before they become crises so that timely adaptations can be implemented (Sylvia & Sylvia, 2012, p. 25). Ultimately, evaluation research can inform and improve the operations of criminal justice programs and enhance service delivery.

Strengths and Weaknesses of Program Evaluation

The evaluation program is both a political and scientific process. The two issues are tied together inextricably. The scientific validity of the study colors and determines the value and objectivity of the research findings and their policy implications. This is "applied" research in that the primary objective of program evaluation is to determine whether the crime prevention program is reaching its goals—defined and desired results.

Evaluation research is different from other research in seven basic ways (Weiss, 1998, pp. 6–8):

1. *Use for decision making:* The results of evaluation research are designed with use in mind. The evaluation should provide a basis for decision making in the future and provide information to determine whether a program should be continued and expanded or terminated.
2. *Program-derived questions:* The research questions are derived from the goals of the program and its operations and are defined by the evaluator alone. The core of the study is administrative and operational: Is the program accomplishing what it is designed to do? Is it reaching its "target population"—that is, the clients that the program was supposed to serve? Does the program make effective and efficient use of its resources, both physical and financial?
3. *Judgmental quality:* Objectivity requires that the evaluator focuses on whether the program is achieving its desired goals. It is imperative that these goals are stated in a clear and measurable fashion that accurately documents effective performance.

4. *Action setting:* The most important thing going on is the program, not the research. The program administrator and staff control access to information, records, and their clients. The research must deal with this reality and construct research designs that are feasible in the real-world setting.
5. *Role conflicts:* The administrator's priority is providing program services, which often makes him or her unresponsive to the needs of the evaluation. Typically, the administrator believes strongly in the value and worth of the program services. The judgmental nature of the findings and the establishment of accountability are often viewed as a threat to both the program and the administrator personally. The possibility of friction between the program and research and the administrator and evaluator is almost inevitable. Programs are often tied to both the ego and professional reputation of the administrator and staff. Some programs (e.g., Drug Abuse Resistance Education, or D.A.R.E.) are politically attractive, and as a result have lives of their own that defy objectivity and rational assessment. Negative outcomes are not always accepted in a rational manner. In fact, one of the great ironies of evaluation research is that negative findings often fail to kill a program and positive results seldom save one. This is due to the fact that so many crime prevention programs are tied to availability of grant funding. The presence or absence of funding often determines program survival regardless of the program evaluation research findings.
6. *Publication:* Publication of evaluation research is vital to the establishment of a base of information on effective crime prevention programs. To be published, the research must be carefully designed and executed and the statistical analysis must be valid and accurate.
7. *Allegiance:* The evaluator is clearly conflicted on this aspect. He or she has obligations to the organization that funds the study, to the scientific requirements of research objectivity, and to work for the betterment of society through the determination of program effectiveness. These obligations can be contradictory and the researcher must face this reality. For example, program officials often need real-time assessments of tactics as they unfold. If the evaluator discovers problems during the process evaluation of program implementation that might jeopardize its success, then the evaluator has an obligation to alert program officials without compromising ethical concerns (Joyce & Ramsey, 2013, p. 361).

Thus, research findings have utility in that they can guide future programming and crime policy. However, the results of evaluation research are not always clear and unequivocal, even when the research design is valid and vital. Findings are often small in magnitude and effect and may be influenced by forces (both social and political) that cannot be isolated from those of the program itself. Thus, program administrators and policy makers typically consider the evaluation research results in combination with other factors such as public opinion, cost, availability of staff and facilities, and possible alternatives (Weiss, 1998, pp. 3–4).

Determination of effectiveness is the crucial difficulty facing the evaluator. The practical problems of obtaining valid data and faithfully executing the research design often conflict with the realities of operating the crime prevention program. The evaluator never has complete control over the research process because of the need to administer the program. Program operations drive the evaluation and its design. The relationship between the needs of the evaluation and the program must be continually balanced. Ultimately, the evaluation research design must be flexible enough to address this relationship. Cooperation between the program administrator and evaluator must be firmly established and maintained. The research must be tied to the changing nature of daily program operations.

The ultimate aim of evaluation research is to guide rational policy making that is based on valid research findings. The rationale is that programs that have been deemed effective will be expanded to other areas and locations and those that fail will be terminated and abandoned. In recent years, evidence-based best practices have grown significantly. Here, the emphasis is on rationality. Ideally, there should be a systematic, evidence-based foundation for criminal justice policies and programs that will increase both the accountability and effectiveness of the criminal justice system (Mears, 2010, p. 2). The search for what works has extended across all areas of the criminal justice system (both adult and juvenile)—police, courts, and corrections.

Evidence-Based Practices

One form of analysis that categorizes, analyzes, and summarizes the research information on a particular criminal justice policy or program is the *systematic review*. Systematic reviews "use rigorous methods to locate, appraise, and synthesize findings from criminal justice program evaluation studies. Typically, they give their criteria for including studies, conduct an extensive search to find them, code their key features (especially their methodology), and provide conclusions of their review" (Welch & Farrington, 2001, p. 161).

For example, Braga (2001) conducted a traditional, narrative review of studies of the effects of hot-spot policing on crime. He reviewed nine studies—five randomized experiments and four nonequivalent control group quasi-experiments. Overall, the research findings revealed that focused police efforts (aggressive disorder enforcement, directed patrols, proactive arrests, and problem solving) can prevent crime in high-risk places that feature concentrations of crime without resulting in crime displacement effects. However, the study was unable to determine exactly what types of police interventions are most preferable in controlling crime at hot-spot locations.

Maryland Report

Probably the most pertinent example of a systematic review is the "Maryland Report." This report was written in response to a request from the U.S. Congress to review existing research on criminal justice programs and identify those determined to be most effective (Sherman et al., 1997, p. 4). The report reviewed more than 500 crime prevention program evaluations and classified them according to both their scientific methodology and their research findings to establish a list of program effectiveness (i.e., what works, what doesn't work, and what is promising). Their "Maryland scale of scientific methods" rested primarily on three factors (Sherman et al., 1998, p. 4):

- Control of other variables that might have been the true causes of any connection between the program and crime.
- Measurement error from such matters as loss of subjects over time or low interview response rates.
- Statistical power to detect the magnitude of program effects.

The authors also classified evaluation reports according to five additional research design criteria, which are listed in Table 1.1.

The methodological rigor of the research increases with each category level and enhances the validity of the findings. These concepts will be discussed in detail in Chapter 6.

"What Works"

The authors of the "Maryland Report" used this research-based classification system to identify programs in three categories: "What Works," "What's Promising," and "What Doesn't Work." Several programs were designated under the category "What Works." In particular, family and parent training was identified as an effective intervention for delinquents and adolescents at risk for delinquency. Coaching of high-risk youth in thinking skills was effective in treating high-risk youth in schools. For adults, vocational training yielded excellent results for older, male ex-offenders, thus stressing the need to provide jobs after incarceration. For convicted offenders, rehabilitation programs with risk-focused treatments demonstrated promise.

Table 1.1 Research Design Criteria used in the "Maryland Report"

Level	Attributes
1	There is a correlation between a crime prevention program and a measure of crime or crime risk factors at a single point in time.
2	There is a temporal sequence between the program and crime or risk outcome that is clearly observed, or the presence of a comparison group without demonstrated comparability to the treatment group.
3	The research features a comparison of two or more comparable units of analysis, one with and one without the program services.
4	The research features a comparison between multiple units with and without the program, controlling for other factors, or using comparison units that evidence only minor differences.
5	The research features random assignment of comparable units to program and comparison groups.

Source: Sherman et al. (1998), pp. 4–5.

In addition, therapeutic community treatment programs for drug-using offenders were effective while they were incarcerated.

In the area of crime prevention, nuisance abatement action on landlords was designated as a proven method of preventing drug dealing in rental housing. Extra police patrols were effective in dealing with crime "hot spots." Monitoring by specialized police units and incarceration reduced the crime threat posed by high-risk, repeat offenders, while on-scene arrests controlled employed, domestic abusers.

"What's Promising"

Under this category, the authors of the "Maryland Report" noted several programs that the research identified as having a potential impact on crime. With law enforcement, one such policy focuses on proactive drunk-driving arrests with breath testing as a method of combating driving while intoxicated. Community policing programs that provided citizen meetings to set priorities had promising results. Polite field interrogation of suspicious persons by the police had potential crime prevention aspects. Mailing of arrest warrants to domestic violence suspects who leave the scene before the police arrive provided a method of solving a problem after the incident took place. Higher numbers of police officers in cities seemed to impact the crime rate in those cities. Gang monitoring by community workers and probation and police officers provided a potential deterrent effect to prevent gang violence. A police focus on proactive arrests for carrying concealed weapons was also a potential way to prevent violence in communities.

With delinquents, community-based mentoring by Big Brothers/Big Sisters of America and community-based after-school recreation programs helped to stem delinquency. Job Corps residential training programs for at-risk youth offered an alternative, conventional lifestyle to combat delinquency.

For adults, treatment alternatives such as battered women shelters, drug courts, and drug treatment in jails followed by drug testing in the community offered ways to deal with community-based problems that feed the criminal justice system.

In terms of crime prevention, moving urban public housing residents to suburban homes had the potential to protect crime victims and eliminate sites that tend to attract offenders and crime. Using two clerks in already-robbed convenience stores could prevent future victimization. Target-hardening methods such as street closures, barricades, and rerouting streets were also identified as ways to prevent crime through environmental design in neighborhoods.

Under both of the preceding categories, programs that had demonstrated treatment effects were identified for the purpose of spreading their impact. Communities faced with similar problems could implement these programs with a reasonable expectation that they will be effective.

"What Doesn't Work"

Of course, it is also useful to identify crime programs that have proven to be ineffective, such as gun buy-back programs. In particular, the "Maryland Report" identified "sensational" popular programs that the research documented as failures. Initiatives such as D.A.R.E., correctional "boot camps" using traditional military basic training, "scared straight" programs whereby minor juvenile offenders visit adult prisons, shock probation, shock parole, residential programs for juvenile offenders using challenging experiences in rural settings ("wilderness" programs), and split sentences adding jail time to probation or parole failed to provide the deterrent effect to prevent reoffending. Similarly, home detention with electronic monitoring and intensive supervision (ISP) on probation or parole failed to prevent recidivism in community corrections.

Overall, the "Maryland Report" clearly identified some myths and realities about effective crime prevention and treatment programs. The ability of the evaluation results to indicate effectiveness helps to identify programs and policies that can be expanded and have the potential to reduce crime.

Meta-Analysis

Meta-analysis is a more methodologically sophisticated approach to reviewing the literature on a particular intervention (theory, program, or policy) than systematic review. Pratt (2010) defines both the nature and purpose of meta-analysis. It "attempts to integrate the findings of multiple independent tests of a similar hypothesis in a more objective manner by treating the empirical study as the unit of analysis" (Pratt, 2010, p. 154). He likens meta-analysis to the computation of a batting average in baseball. In meta-analysis, the effect size indicates how many hits on average are related to the dependent variable across the studies considered. In addition, the effect size can also reflect the relationships between the independent and dependent variables and across varied methodologies (i.e., longitudinal studies).

In this fashion, meta-analysis provides a distinct advantage over the traditional narrative reviews of an intervention (e.g., the "Maryland Report") where scholars review studies, select them according to rigor of their methodologies, and then interpret the importance of their findings. With regard to program evaluation, its key strategy is to identify all available studies on a policy or program, code their findings and methodologies into objective categories, and then conduct quantitative analysis of these data (Wells, 2009, p. 271). The use of meta-analysis in criminal justice research has grown over time. Wells (2009) identified 176 meta-analysis studies in criminal justice published between 1978 and 2006, with most occurring after 2000. In terms of program evaluation, the majority of these meta-analytic studies (99—56.3% of the total number) were "pragmatic" in nature—that is, assessments of the effectiveness or utility of a practical intervention (Wells, 2009, p. 280).

Meta-analysis provides several distinct differences over traditional reviews of the literature. First, it can provide a single precise estimate of the effect size between two variables, thus providing an indication of the strength of the relationship between them. Second, it is possible to obtain the effect size of the relationship across different methodologies. To control for differences in rigor between methodologies, it is possible to code each study according to its methodology. Third, it makes it possible to consider a subject over time. As new studies on a subject are conducted, they can be added to the meta-analysis (Pratt, 2010, pp. 155–156). Of course, the quality of the meta-analysis is dependent on those of the studies included in the review.

Pratt (2010) also addresses the question of when meta-analysis should be performed. With regard to program evaluation, there are issues here. First, a meta-analysis can clarify the relationship between an intervention and its effectiveness when published studies of it have generated "mixed" results. This is done by considering such factors as the methodological differences across studies as well as the theoretical variables under consideration. Second and most important to us, meta-analysis can assess whether a policy or program "works" across time and places by examining the literature on the intervention and generating an effect size (Pratt, 2010, p. 158). In fact, meta-analysis was invented for this particular purpose—to assess the effectiveness of various treatments and interventions in education, psychology, medicine, and interventions with offenders (Pratt, 2010, p. 160). In criminal justice, meta-analysis makes it possible to assess the effectiveness of a policy or program by synthesizing and quantifying the magnitude of effect size (Wells, 2009, p. 269).

An example of this type of meta-analysis is a study of 66 published and unpublished evaluations of prison-based drug treatment programs (therapeutic communities, residential substance abuse treatment, group counseling, boot camps designed for drug offenders, and narcotic maintenance programs) (Mitchell, et al., 2007). The methodological requirements for inclusion in the analysis were (Mitchell et al., 2007, pp. 356–357):

- The evaluation utilized an experimental design (with a control group) or quasi-experimental design (that included a no-treatment comparison group).
- It measured both post-program drug use and reoffending.
- The research was conducted between 1980 and 2004.
- The evaluation reported enough information to calculate an effect size.

Overall, the research results indicated that prison participants in therapeutic communities had lower rates of post-program drug use and reoffending. Thus, the research on therapeutic communities had the "most consistent evidence of treatment effectiveness" (Mitchell, 2007, p. 369).

Similarly, Shaffer (2011, pp. 500–501) conducted a meta-analysis of 60 studies on drug court treatment programs. The studies were coded along five categories:

1. Study characteristics (e.g., affiliation of authors, type of publication, and publication year).
2. Sample characteristics (e.g., race, gender, age, and criminal history).
3. General program characteristics (e.g., program length, setting, adult/juvenile, year implemented, and graduation rate).
4. Methodological characteristics (e.g., study design, sample size, attrition rate, outcomes, length of follow-up, and statistical power).
5. Outcome characteristics (e.g., type of outcome and calculated effect size).

In addition, the data were coded under 11 categories:
1. Target population (e.g., type of charge, type of offender, and motivation).
2. Assessment (e.g., areas assessed and method of assessment).
3. Leverage (e.g., drug court model, consequences of failure, and benefits of graduation).
4. Philosophy (e.g., view toward substance abuse, primary role of judge, and flexibility of policies regarding rewards and sanctions).
5. Treatment characteristics (e.g., length of treatment, graduation rate, treatment type, treatment targets, and adolescents' participation in Alcoholics Anonymous and Narcotics Anonymous [AA/NA]).
6. Predictability (e.g., system of rewards and punishers and immediacy of response to infractions).
7. Intensity (e.g., average number of contacts and standard conditions and requirements).
8. Service delivery (e.g., single provider, internal provider, and dedicated caseloads).
9. Staff characteristics (e.g., initial training, conference attendance, and team meetings).
10. Funding (e.g., adequate funding and federal funding).
11. Quality assurance (e.g., internal and external QA and advisory board).

Therefore, this study focused on the impact of the policies and procedures of the drug courts upon their effectiveness. The findings of the research indicated that the drug courts were most effective when violent and noncompliant offenders were excluded from the program. Also notable was the fact that pre-plea drug courts were the most effective (Shaffer, 2011, p. 513). Thus, the study provided some information on how drug courts should be operated to achieve optimal results.

In another meta-analysis of drug courts, Mitchell and colleagues (2012) reviewed 154 independent evaluations of drug courts (92 aimed at adults, 34 for juveniles, and 28 that targeted DWI [drinking while intoxicated] offenders). They determined that the adult drug court participants had lower recidivism rates than nonparticipants—from 38% to 50% less with the treatment effect lasting three years. However, the DWI clients did not seem to be as effective, and juvenile drug courts had an even smaller impact upon recidivism.

These studies demonstrate how meta-analysis can provide focused results on the strength of the effectiveness of criminal justice programs. They also considered the quality of the research and the nature of the intervention in their analyses. This type of information is particularly relevant to decision makers.

Campbell Collaboration (Crime and Justice Group)

A more recent development to promote the creation of valid evaluation research is the *Campbell Collaboration*. Named for experimental psychologist and noted methodologist Donald T. Campbell, the collaboration was established to prepare, maintain, and disseminate evidence-based research on the effects of interventions in education, social welfare, and crime and justice. Like the "Maryland Report," the Campbell Collaboration sponsors and encourages the development of rigorous and valid evaluation reports that can contribute to the policy-making process. In particular, it's Crime and Justice Group aims to prepare and maintain systematic reviews of crime programs and policies and make them electronically accessible through its website (*http://www.campbellcollaboration.org/crime_and_justice/index.php*) to all concerned parties. The Crime and Justice Group also promotes the establishment of methodological criteria for including studies in their reviews, securing research funding, and making the best knowledge about the effectiveness of crime programs and policies available to all (Farrington & Petrosino 2001).

The website provides abstracts of reports and articles on crime prevention programs. For example, 35 manuscripts were listed on the website at the time of writing this book. Many of the studies were on programs listed under the "Maryland Report," such as hot-spot policing, drug courts, domestic violence, and early family/parent training programs. However, recent crime prevention target-hardening techniques were also reviewed, including the effects of improved street lighting and closed-circuit television surveillance on crime. Offender treatment programs, such as mentoring programs for juveniles, were also identified.

Summary

In this chapter, we introduced the purpose of criminal justice programs evaluation. In their most valid form, the results of a program evaluation can provide information for decision makers to guide criminal justice policy in a rational manner. Systematic reviews and meta-analyses of criminal justice program evaluations help to inform this process. The recent efforts of the "Maryland Report" and the Campbell Collaboration (Crime and Justice Group) have enhanced the ability of evaluation research to achieve these goals.

The emphasis of program evaluation is clearly on accountability. In the words of the "Maryland Report," we want to know what works—that is, policies and programs that effectively prevent crime and delinquency. The rigorous testing of crime prevention programs through valid research methods in program evaluation will assure us that information and knowledge about these efforts will be provided and, hopefully, disseminated to practitioners and the public.

Discussion Questions

1. Review and discuss the strengths and weaknesses of program evaluation.
2. How did the "Maryland Report" determine how research on criminal justice programs should be evaluated?
3. In the "Maryland Report," what programs demonstrated evidence that they worked, did not work, or were promising?
4. What are the aims of the Campbell Collaboration?
5. Why is it important to determine what works in criminal justice? How do systematic reviews and meta-analyses help to determine program effectiveness?

References

Adams, S. (1975). *Evaluative research in corrections: A practical guide*. Washington, D.C.: U.S. Department of Justice.

Braga, A. (2001). The Effects of Hot Spots Policing on Crime. *Annals of the American Academy of Political and Social Science, 578*, 104–125.

Farrington, D. P., & Petrosino, A. (2001). The campbell collaboration crime and justice group. *The Annals of the Academy of Political and Social Science, 578*, 35–49.

Joyce, N. M., & Ramsey, C. H. (2013). Commentary on smart policing. *Police Quarterly, 16*(3), 358–368.

Lipsey, M. W. (2005). *Improving the evaluation of anticrime programs: Committee on improving evaluation of anticrime programs*. Washington, DC: The National Academies Press.

Mitchell, O., Wilson, D. B., & MacKenzie, D. L. (2007). Does Incarceration-based Drug Treatment Reduce Recidivism? A Meta-Analytic Synthesis of the Research. *Journal of Experimental Criminology, 3*, 353–375.

Mears, D. P. (2010). *American criminal justice policy: An evaluation approach to increasing accountability and effectiveness*. New York: Cambridge University Press.

Mitchell, O., Wilson, D. B., Eggers, A., & MacKenzie, D. L. (2012). Assessing the effectiveness of drug courts on recidivism: A meta-analytic review of traditional and nontraditional drug courts. *Journal of Criminal Justice, 40*(1), 60–71.

Mitchell, O., Wilson, D. B., & MacKenzie, D. L. (2007). Does incarceration-based drug treatment reduce recidivism? a meta-analytic synthesis of the research. *Journal of Experimental Criminology, 3*, 353–375.

Pratt, T. C. (2010). Meta-analysis in criminal justice and criminology: What it is, when it's useful, and what to watch out for. *Journal of Criminal Justice Education, 21*(2), 152–167.

Shaffer, D. K. (2011). Looking inside the black box of drug courts: A meta-analytic review. *Justice Quarterly, 28*(3), 493–521.

Sherman, L., Gottfredson, D., MacKenzie, D., Eck, J., Reuter, P., & Bushway, S. (1997). *Preventing crime: What works, what doesn't, what's promising: A report to the united states congress*. Washington, DC: National Institute of Justice.

Sherman, L., Gottfredson, D., MacKenzie, D., Eck, J., Reuter, P., & Bushway, S. D. (1998). *National institute of justice research in brief: What works, what doesn't, what's promising.* Washington, DC: National Institute of Justice.

Suchman, E. A. (1974). *Evaluative research: Principles and practice in public service and social action programs.* New York: Russell Sage Foundation.

Sylvia, R. D., & Sylvia, K. M. (2012). *Program evaluation and planning for the public manager.* Long Grove, IL: Waveland Press.

Weiss, C. (1998). *Evaluation research: Methods for assessing program effectiveness.* Englewood Cliffs, NJ: Prentice-Hall.

Welch, B. C., & Farrington, D. P. (2001). Toward an evidence-based approach of preventing crime. *The Annals of the American Academy of Political and Social Science, 578,* 158–173.

Wells, E. (2009). The uses of meta-analysis in criminal justice research: A quantitative review. *Justice Quarterly, 26*(2), 268–294.

PLANNING A PROGRAM EVALUATION

Keywords
problem-oriented policing (POP)
SARA
S.M.A.R.T.
logic model

CHAPTER OUTLINE
Introduction   15
Problem-Oriented Policing   16
Planning an Evaluation Strategy   18
   Goal Setting: S.M.A.R.T.   18
   Goal–Objective Relationship   19
   Develop Evaluation Measures   19
   Data Collection   20
   Determine Analysis Methods   21
Logic Model   22
Politics of Evaluation Research   24
Ethical Issues in Evaluation Research   25
   Ethics of Conducting Research   25
   Ethics and Social Relationships in Evaluation Research   28
Summary   29
Discussion Questions   29
References   30

Planning proceeds step by step and each step must be evaluated before the next step can be taken.
—**Edward Suchman (1987)**

Introduction

Criminal justice programs are designed to address a particular need and solve a defined problem. Crime problems are often intractable and difficult to address. Strategic thinking, planning, and operations are required to address the sources of crime problems, both individual and systemic. Panaceas and "silver-bullet" solutions to crime problems are often sought but never found. Collection of data and the compilation of research evidence typically are a part of program evaluation.

This is where program planning begins and program evaluation follows. This process has been adequately summarized under the problem-oriented policing (POP) acronym (SARA) (Goldstein, 1990):

- *Scanning:* Identify recurring problems and how they affect community safety.
- *Analysis:* Determine the causes of the problem.
- *Response:* Seeking out, selecting, and implementing activities to solve the problem.
- *Assessment:* Determine if the response was effective or identify new strategies.

The aim of this process is to collect data that are related to the problem, determine the validity of these data, trace causal relationships that could lead to problem identification and program development to address the problem, and then determine if the program was effective in solving the problem.

Scanning involves looking for and identifying problems. The initial analysis is made to determine if a problem exists and whether a detailed analysis is required to uncover it. Problems are also prioritized and personnel allocated.

Analysis is concerned with learning about the causes, scope, and effects of the problem. Who are the actors involved in the problem (both offenders and victims)? What are the specific incidents of the problem and what is the sequence of events leading to it? What responses have been made by the community and government agencies?

Response involves acting to alleviate the problem. Planned solutions can be organized regarding total elimination of the problem, material reduction of the problem, reduction of the harm caused by the problem, using the best possible solution to the problem, and even removing the problem from police consideration.

Assessment is where program evaluation comes in. That is, did the response work?

Problem-Oriented Policing

POP requires that the police develop a systematic process for examining and addressing the problems that the public expects them to handle. It requires identifying these problems in more precise terms, researching each problem, documenting the nature of the current police response, assessing its adequacy and the adequacy of existing authority and resources, engaging in a broad exploration of alternatives to present responses, weighing the merits of these alternatives, and choosing from among them (Goldstein, 1979).

As defined by the San Diego, CA, police department (Capowich & Roehl, 1994, pp. 127–128):

> *POP emphasizes identifying and analyzing problems (criminal, civil, or public nuisance) and implementing solutions to resolve the underlying causes of the problem. It emphasizes proactive intervention rather than reactive responses to calls for service, resolution of root causes rather than symptoms, and use of multiparty, community-based problem solving rather than a unilateral police response. POP focuses on a problem in a long-term, comprehensive manner, rather than handling the problem as a series of separate incidents to be resolved via arrest or other police action.*

In San Diego, the police focused on street robberies for one year. Research determined that calls for service did not decrease over the one-year period. Yet, the indicators revealed that the POP approach improved the circumstances for those who used the stations and reduced the police workload at those stations. However, the role played by citizen groups in this project was very limited.

Elsewhere, research on POP reports positive results. In both Newport News, VA, and Baltimore County, MD, officers concentrated on underlying causes of crime. They collected information and enlisted the support of public and private agencies. As a result, both crime and fear of crime were substantially reduced in both areas (Eck & Spelman, 1987). The Center for Problem-Oriented Policing provides copies of evaluations (*www.popcenter.org/casestudies/*) of POP operations that have effectively addressed such disparate problems as drunken driving, repeat sex offenders, construction site thefts, thefts from cars in parking facilities, burglary of single-family houses, drug dealing in apartment complexes, loud car stereos, street prostitution, and residential speeding.

Basically, there are two ways to define a policing problem. In clear terms, a policing problem exists when something is going wrong for someone somewhere and somebody wants the police to do something about it. Problems can be perceived as a group of events that are similar in one or more ways that are harmful to members of the public and that citizens expect the police to handle.

The problem analysis process must ferret out relationships among the variables collected in the data to determine the extent and nature of the problem. It is also important to ascertain if the problem can be adequately measured and thus serve as the basis for an outcome evaluation. First, there are concerns regarding the data: Can adequate data be obtained? Second, there are resource questions to be addressed: Does the police have the tools necessary to collect data and analyze it? What amount of time and money are necessary to conduct the study? Hopefully, the problem addressed is significant enough to advance knowledge and practice in criminal justice and the analysis will contribute to future attempts to address the problem in question. In this manner, evaluation research not only examines the effectiveness of a particular program or policy, but also adds to crime prevention knowledge by revealing those strategies that have proven to be able to solve a crime problem.

Planning an Evaluation Strategy

The program evaluator must first develop a plan to conduct the research process. Basically, evaluation planning involves the completion of five basic steps:

1. State the goals of the program in clear and measurable (quantifiable) terms.
2. Determine the relationship between goals and objectives.
3. Develop evaluation measures.
4. Determine the data to be collected on these measures.
5. Determine analysis methods.

These steps help clarify the aims and abilities of the program in question to address the crime problem.

Goal Setting: S.M.A.R.T.

Program goals are not often stated in clear terms, and they often express the wishes of a particular group rather than a definite target. They are not stated in a manner that will make it possible to determine whether the program is effective. Here, the evaluator attempts to state the goals of the program in measurable terms that indicate their achievement. They are often stated as a percentage to be attained over a specified time period. They should be attainable, reasonable, and reflect what can be achieved if the program is effective. For example, the goal of a burglary prevention program could be stated in measurable terms as: To reduce the number of reported burglaries in the target area by 25% over a one-year period. Note that this statement indicates what the unit of measurement is (the number of reported burglaries) as well as the percentage target (25%) and the time period (one year after the program begins). However, what is the basis for such an expectation? Has previous research on burglary prevention programs revealed that a 25% reduction is possible? If the target specified by the goal is unrealistic and unattainable, its use as a performance benchmark is worthless.

One method to avoid these problems in goal setting is to follow the acronym S.M.A.R.T, as shown in Figure 2.1. (see Locke & Latham, 2013). Well-defined goals should be:

- *Specific:* Goals must be clear and specific. They should represent what the program is trying to accomplish and accurately measure successful operations.

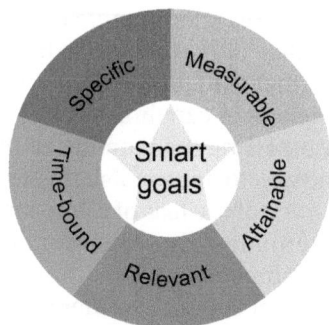

Figure 2.1 S.M.A.R.T. goals.

- *Measureable:* If the goal is not measurable, there is no way to gauge progress.
- *Attainable:* Again, goals must be realistic. Some effort and stretching is always in order, but goals should neither be too high or too low so they become meaningless.
- *Relevant:* The goals should represent and mirror the vision and mission of the program.
- *Time-bound:* Goals must have starting and end points and the duration of the measurement should be stated clearly.

Formulating goals in this fashion will ensure good performance by letting stakeholders know what is expected of them. Of course, they will also guide the course of the impact evaluation.

Goal–Objective Relationship

In terms of our example, the burglary prevention program is designed to reduce the incidence of this type of crime in the geographic area served by the program. This analysis can be extended to compare the incidence of burglary citywide in the areas not served by the program.

Develop Evaluation Measures

The next step is to identify the evaluation measures for the program under consideration – in this instance, a burglary prevention program. Here, the measures can take three basic forms:
- *Effectiveness:* These measures determine the degree of success of the program in dealing with the problem at hand. Here, we have stated that the quantifiable goal of the burglary prevention program is to reduce the incidence of reported burglaries in the targeted area by 25% over a one-year period.

- *Efficiency:* These measures should indicate how well the program has been implemented and whether it has been implemented according to the original plan for the program.
- *Attitudinal:* These measures can indicate whether the program has been successful by assessing the attitudes of the program's clients. In our example, one way to accomplish this would be to conduct a before-and-after survey of the fear of crime among residents of the targeted area to determine if they felt safer after the burglary prevention program was implemented.

In addition, the evaluator should consider the impact of factors that occurred during the implementation of the program that could also affect these measures. For example, if the state in which the burglary prevention program was implemented passed a "rob a house, go to prison" (i.e., mandatory incarceration) bill, it may have an impact on the incidence of the number of reported burglaries.

Valid performance measures should have the following characteristics. First, they should be credible—accurate and relevant representations of both the quality and quantity of services provided by the program. Second, they should provide a fair indication of program performance and reflect the factors and operations that program administrators can truly influence and control. Third, they should be clear—easy to utilize and comprehend and practical to administer and implement.

Data Collection

The fourth step in this process is to determine the data necessary to perform the evaluation, the constraints on their availability, how these data will be collected and managed, and a method to determine the validity of these measures. In terms of understanding the problem that the proposed program addresses, four strategies are recommended for the evaluator (Bickman, Rog, & Hedrick, 1998, p. 7):

- Hold discussions with research clients or sponsors to obtain the clearest possible picture of their concerns.
- Review the relevant literature on the subject.
- Gather current information from experts and major interested parties on the issue.
- Conduct information-gathering visits and observations to obtain a real-world sense of the context, and talk with persons actively involved in the issue.

In our example, it will be necessary to determine the baseline level of reported burglaries in the target area prior to program implementation and then the same measure after the program has been in place for one year. It will be necessary for the evaluator to establish methods to obtain these measures from the police department in question and to determine how they collect and report information on reported burglaries in their jurisdiction. The evaluator must determine if these measures are valid indicators of the incidence of burglaries in the area or whether it will be necessary to conduct a victimization survey of homes in the target area. Such a survey could determine whether burglaries occurred that were not reported to the police as well as the previously mentioned assessment of the fear of crime in the area (both before and after the program was implemented).

The cost of obtaining these data must also be considered by the evaluator. Obtaining the data from the police is much less costly than the possible victimization survey of homes in the target area. Burglary data would be regularly collected by the police, but the survey must be conducted by the evaluator. In any event, the evaluator must design an information system to collect all forms of data required by the program evaluation in a format that is amenable to statistical analysis and computerized. The availability of computers (tablet, laptop, or desktop) and statistical analysis programs (Excel, SPSS, SAS) helps to simplify this task.

Data must be carefully collected with an eye toward quality control. Procedures to collect the data must be established and variables must be explicitly defined in measurable terms so that the meaning of the data is clear and will be followed carefully. The source of the data must be clearly identified, and the process of data storage, maintenance, and processing must be specified.

Determine Analysis Methods

The final step is the determination of quantitative and/or qualitative methods of analysis that will be utilized in the evaluation. These methods will be determined in part by the evaluation design, the type of evaluation measures used, and their validity and reliability. The evaluator should consider how the evaluation measures will be calculated and if these measures can be combined.

In our burglary prevention program example, a before-and-after comparison of the number and rate of reported burglaries before and one year after program implementation in terms of the expressed target of a 25% reduction is a rather simple comparison. However, other points of comparison could be added by conducting the same method of analysis for the areas of the city not served by the program. In addition, the evaluator could conduct a regression analysis based on past levels of reported burglaries to determine whether the number of reported burglaries after the one-year period of implementation compared to the expected number of reported burglaries calculated by the regression analysis. In addition, the proposed victimization survey could provide another level of comparison by asking the respondents in the area their experiences with burglary victimization over the time period in question, as well as their fear of crime over this period.

One of the mechanisms used to display and describe the underlying theory and purpose of a program prior to conducting program evaluation is the use of a logic model.

Logic Model

The process of establishing goals, objectives, and performance indicators requires that the theory that provides the basis for the program must be specified. In turn, the theory informs program operations by:
- Driving the selection of treatments.
- Clarifying the description of the services provided to clients with defined needs.
- Helping to determine what variables need to be measured.
- Driving how one interprets a simple comparison of the outcomes of two programs to deeper analyses in terms of research on the topical area in general.

These are also the elements of the logic model of a program—the framework that shows how the program might theoretically produce the desired outcomes and impacts (Boruch, 1998, p. 172).

The logic model specifies the conceptual framework of an evaluation by establishing the variables to be measured and the expected relationships among them. The logic model provides an explanation of how the program is expected to work and how the program goals, processes, resources, and outcomes will provide the direction for the program. Thus, they provide a clear "roadmap" of what is planned and expected results—a review of the strength of the connection between activities and outcomes (Knowlton & Phillips, 2013, p. 5). As a diagram, the logic model demonstrates the cause-and-effect mechanism between how the program will meet certain needs to achieve desired outcomes (Davidson, 2005, p. 38). It focuses the evaluation of the program's effectiveness and can communicate changes in its implementation over the life of the program (Bickman et al., 1998, p. 8).

Table 2.1 presents a logic model for adult drug court programs as proposed by the National Institute of Justice. First is the program inputs, the resources required to operate the program. Then, the program activities are the components of the program. Next, program outputs indicate the work done and the results of activities. Finally, related to outcomes are the short-term and long-term outcomes that represent the objectives of the program. Note that both the short-term and long-term program outcomes are measures of program performance for which data must be collected and compiled on program operations and activities. Thus, they will serve as the basis for the assessment of program performance and must be collected in a timely

Table 2.1 Adult Drug Court Program Logic Model

Inputs	Activities	Outputs	Short-Term Outcomes	Long-Term Outcomes	External Factors
Probation	Risk/needs assessments	Program intake screen	Recidivism in-program	Recidivism post-program	Community
Community	Judicial interaction	Program admission	Alcohol and other drug use in-program	Alcohol and other drug use post-program	Legal/penal code
Public resources	Alcohol and other drug monitoring (including testing)	Court appearances	Supervision violation	Program/ graduation termination	Courthouse
Courthouse	Community supervision	Treatment admission	Program violation	Probation revocation/ successful termination	
Treatment	Graduated sanctions or incentives (including jail)	Alcohol and other drug tests	Treatment retention	Jail/prison imposed	
Jail	Alcohol and other drug treatment services	Probation contracts	Skills development	Employment, education, housing, and health	
Grant funds	Ancillary services	Classes attended	Service needs met		
Technical assistance		Services accessed	Criminal thinking		
		Jail stays			

Source: National Institute of Justice, http://www.nij.gov/topics/courts/drug-courts/full-logic-model.htm.

fashion—hopefully in a computer-based information system operated and maintained by the adult drug court program. The external factors listed in Table 2 refer to outside forces that can affect the drug court program. For example, both the community and the courthouse work group could oppose or support the creation of a drug court. In addition, the legal/penal code of the state must be consulted to determine if the operations of the drug court are permissable.

By specifying the relationships among these key factors, the logic model clarifies why the program was adopted and how it is expected to work. Thus, it serves as a blueprint for the evaluation of the effectiveness of the program.

Politics of Evaluation Research

Up to this point, we have presented a rational model of program evaluation. But it must be stressed that programs are political animals. The reputations and egos of program sponsors and administrators are tied to the success of the proposed program. It is unlikely that these groups will approach the evaluation in an experimental fashion. Thus, the evaluator must navigate through some treacherous territory, trying to maintain research accuracy and validity while measuring program performance in a fair fashion.

One of the founders of evaluation research, Dr. Donald T. Campbell, examined the differences between "trapped" and "experimental" administrators. A trapped administrator is committed to the relevance and significance of the program. Therefore, if the evaluation research findings are critical or negative, a trapped administrator will feel threatened and will be inclined to question the validity of the research, regardless of previous involvement in the development of the evaluation process. An experimental administrator has a decidedly broader view and is committed to the improvement of public policy rather than the promotion of a particular program. If the program under review is found to be ineffective, an experimental administrator will be disappointed but ready to plan a new initiative to address the problem at hand. This administrator is thus pragmatic, thinking strategically about improving public policy rather than defending a failed program (Campbell, 1969).

The answers that the program administrator seeks from program evaluation can be specified as follows (Behn, 2003, p. 588):

- *Evaluate:* How well is my agency performing?
- *Control:* How can I ensure that my subordinates are doing the right thing?
- *Manage the budget:* On what programs, people, or projects should my agency spend the public's money?
- *Motivate:* How can I motivate line staff, middle managers, nonprofit, and for-profit collaborators, stakeholders, and citizens to do the things necessary to improve performance?
- *Promote:* How can I convince political superiors, legislators, stakeholders, journalists, and citizens that my agency is doing a good job?
- *Celebrate:* What accomplishments are worthy of the important organizational ritual of celebrating success?
- *Learn:* How will I know why a program is working or not?
- *Improve:* What exactly should be done differently to improve performance?

But, once again, these purposes reflect rational motives. A trapped administrator can seek to use the program evaluation for illegitimate purposes (Weiss, 1998). He or she may seek to use the evaluation to postpone and delay a difficult decision by conducting the evaluation before making one. He or she may use the evaluation results to duck responsibility for performance. Finally, evaluations are often conducted because they are required by the funding agency's grant requirements and program administrators may view this as an obligation that serves no true purpose for them.

Regardless of these perceptions, the evaluator must attempt to create a climate for the research that maintains the priorities necessary for reliable and relevant findings that can credibly inform public policy. There must be continuous interaction between the evaluator and program administrators to promote an exchange of ideas that will lead to the best possible evaluation process. The evaluator must be especially careful not to overreact to both positive and negative findings and to instead interpret them in a constructive, neutral, and realistic manner. Program administrators should have input in the research process to ensure accurate and realistic measurement of program performance while prohibiting their strict control over the research results. The evaluator must address these issues with program administrators throughout the entire process of program evaluation to keep everyone aware of their rightful roles in the enterprise. Similarly, Carol Weiss (1998) advises evaluators to determine who initiated the idea of conducting a program evaluation and for what purposes. She recommends an examination of the commitment among program administrators to use the results of the evaluation to improve decision making in the future.

Ethical Issues in Evaluation Research

Ethical issues in program evaluation can be divided into two related areas: those relating to the conduct of the research and the other to how the evaluator responds to the social nature of program evaluation.

Ethics of Conducting Research

Ethics refers to how the proposed evaluation research conforms to professional standards of what is "right" and "wrong." The ultimate aim is to prevent harm to research subjects while promoting a research design that will generate valid and relevant results that will help inform public policy. It is often a difficult balance to maintain, but protection of human subjects must remain paramount over the need for scientific knowledge. The basic issue is whether there is potential harm to research participants and whether or not this outweighs the potential benefits of the study. Additionally, the evaluation researcher must make ethical decisions in analyzing the data and reporting the research findings. The evaluation research may face political pressure to report findings in a certain "acceptable" way—that is, minimizing negative

Table 2.2 Guiding Principles for Evaluators

A. *Systematic inquiry:* Evaluators conduct systematic, data-based inquiries.
B. *Competence:* Evaluators provide competent performance to stakeholders.
C. *Integrity/honesty:* Evaluators display honesty and integrity in their own behavior, and attempt to ensure the honesty and integrity of the entire evaluation process.
D. *Respect for people:* Evaluators respect the security, dignity, and self-worth of respondents, program participants, and other evaluation stakeholders.
E. *Responsibilities for general and public welfare:* Evaluators articulate and take into account the diversity of general and public interests and values that may be related to the evaluation.

Source: American Evaluation Association, http://www.eval.org/publications/GuidingPrinciplesPrintable.asp.

results (a "whitewash") and emphasizing positive ones. Either way, significant findings should not be minimized or compromised.

Table 2.2 lists the five ethical principles adopted by the American Evaluation Association (AEA, 2004). These principles are intended to guide the professional practice of evaluators and to inform evaluation clients and the public about what ethical principles evaluators should follow and uphold. These five principles provide an ethical framework within which criminal justice program evaluation should be conducted.

Principle A has to do with systematic inquiry and the methodology of evaluation. Evaluators should utilize methods that have the highest technical standards that are appropriate to the questions and subjects of the evaluations. They should answer questions clearly and present their methodology and analysis techniques in sufficient detail to permit understanding to allow others to interpret and critique their work. As noted in Chapter 1, such detail allowed researchers to make the assessment of what works that was detailed in the "Maryland Report."

Principle B discusses the competence of evaluators. They should possess the technical skills, background, and education to perform the research tasks required by the evaluation. In addition, evaluators should reflect "cultural competence"—awareness of their own culturally based assumptions, their understanding of the diverse worldviews of the participants and stakeholders in the evaluation, and the use of appropriate evaluation methods in working with culturally diverse groups with regard to race, ethnicity, gender, religion, socioeconomics, or other factors relevant to the program evaluation.

Principle C calls for the integrity and honesty of evaluators. Evaluators should honestly negotiate with clients and stakeholders regarding the costs of the research, the tasks to be undertaken (especially data collection and maintenance), the limitations of the methodology, the scope of the results obtained, and the uses of the data from the evaluation. Before the research is undertaken, evaluators should reveal any and all potential conflicts of interest they may have with their role as evaluator. If any changes in originally negotiated plans are made, evaluators should record why they were made and how they may significantly affect the scope and results of the research. Clients and stakeholders should be informed of these changes in a timely fashion. Evaluators should explicitly divulge their own, the client's, and the stakeholders' interests and values in conducting the evaluation. They should not misrepresent the methodology or data findings of the research, as well as attempt to prevent the misuse of their research by others. Finally, evaluators should fully disclose the limitations of the research findings and the source of funding and of the request for the evaluation.

Principle D calls for the respect for people. Evaluators should be aware of the contextual factors that may influence the results of a study, including geographic location, timing, political and social climate, economic conditions, and other relevant activities occurring simultaneously. Evaluators must adhere to traditional social science ethical principles regarding the protection of human subjects, including:

- *Anonymity:* The data obtained for the evaluation must not to be matched to an individual participant. No one, including the researcher, should able to determine who in the sample or population participated in the study and, if an individual did participate, what his or her responses were.
- *Confidentiality:* This guarantees that the relationship will not be identified in any written or verbal communication. Data may be analyzed individually or in aggregate, but when the data are reported, no identifying characteristics should allow for individual-level data/responses to be matched with a participant.
- *Disclosure:* The full disclosure of potential harm to subjects in a proposed evaluation should be provided upfront. While the harm or potential harm to subjects that may follow from research is not intentional, the researcher must be aware of the potential consequences and make decisions as a means of resolving the conflict associated with the potential for harm. This is especially pertinent to criminal behavior where the potential harm to subjects is increased.

Evaluators should seek to maximize the benefits and minimize any unnecessary harm that might occur provided that these procedures do not compromise the integrity of the evaluation findings. Evaluators must carefully judge the costs and benefits of performing certain evaluation procedures and anticipate them during initial negotiations for the evaluation. Finally, the results of the evaluation should be presented in a way that respects the dignity, self-worth, and diversity of the stakeholders, and to account for such differences in the planning, conduct, analysis, and reporting of program evaluation findings.

Principle E upholds the evaluator's responsibilities for the general and public welfare. In the planning and reporting of evaluations, evaluators should include the relevant perspectives and interests of the full range of stakeholders, including not only the immediate operations and outcomes for the program but also their implications and potential side effects. Access should be given to the results of the evaluation with the dissemination of results provided in a clear fashion that promotes understanding of the policy implications of the research findings to not only the stakeholders but to society as a whole.

In sum, these principles were promoted and adopted to stimulate discussion of the proper practice of evaluation, to resolve potential problems that arise during the planning and conduct of the research, and to guide the practice of evaluation.

Ethics and Social Relationships in Evaluation Research

The evaluation researcher must confront the nature of his or her relationship not only with the subjects of the research but first with the program administrators and staff. There is a fine line between operating as an evaluator and a consultant. The evaluator must maintain an independent and objective stance but may be called on to offer advice about program operations as it is designed, implemented, and becomes operational. Feedback on program construction and operations is an important role for the evaluation researcher. The question here is: Can the evaluator play these related roles while maintaining objectivity about program performance? Is it ethical not to offer advice that could improve program operations and performance to maintain research objectivity?

As a program develops and progresses, the evaluation researcher will develop personal ties with program administrators and staff that may make it difficult to deliver "bad news" about program performance. Such relationships are important for professionalism but, again, independence and objectivity must be maintained if the researcher is to maintain credibility. The relationship between the evaluator and the program staff and administration is a symbiotic one. After all, the evaluator has been hired because of his or her scientific expertise in research methodology and data analysis. This knowledge will ensure the validity of the research findings. But the staff and administration are the "experts" in terms of the service provided by the program. They have the knowledge and experience in program substance and delivery that is needed to properly inform the program evaluation, which can lead to the accurate and valid measurement of program goals and the interpretation of research results in a grounded and realistic way. Together, the evaluator and program staff and administration can offer their specific expertise to each other in a way that maximizes the integrity of the research while not compromising independence and objectivity. After all, both groups must be able to deal with and accept the consequences of the research findings and outcomes. As Weiss (1998) has dutifully indicated, the evaluator must be able to live with the study, its uses, and his or her conscience at the same time.

Another aspect that is unique about program evaluation is that the evaluator is typically a contract researcher who has been hired to perform the task of program evaluation. Most often, the evaluation is funded by public financing through grant funding. Typically, the program evaluator is part of the team that writes the initial grant proposal because program evaluation is a component of the grant requirements. One of the guidelines used by the funding agency in the decision to fund a proposal is the quality of the proposed evaluation design. Once funded, the research contract can lead to several misinterpretations and ethical difficulties. First, the existence of a contract often clouds the issue of who owns the research work and results—the funding agency, the program administration, or the evaluator? These issues must be resolved as soon as possible—ideally, before the research is undertaken. Also, as previously noted, the uncertainty of the findings can affect the program administrators in negative ways. They are often unsure of what they are looking for from the evaluation research other than the natural desire for a positive result and endorsement of the program (Inciardi & Siegal, 1981, pp. 170-171). Finally, it must be stressed that the evaluator must maintain both independence and objectivity. In the end, the service provided is "paid for" but the research results are not "bought."

Summary

Careful planning for a program evaluation includes attention to methodology, analysis, and implementation, as well as social and political issues. Evaluators must be attentive to how the proposed research will affect all stakeholders while maintaining professional integrity and independence and meeting the requirements of social science research. This means that both methodological and social issues must be addressed continuously throughout the process of evaluation research.

Discussion Questions

1. What is problem-oriented policing and how does the SARA model demonstrate the need for planning in evaluation research?

2. Why is it important to state evaluation goals in measurable terms? What are the obstacles to this task and how can evaluators overcome them?
3. Define and discuss the elements of a logic model for program evaluation.
4. Discuss the problems raised by the politics of evaluation research.
5. Discuss all of the ethical principles established by the AEA and why they are important.

References

American Evaluation Association (2004, July). *Publications*. Retrieved January 27, 2013, from American Evaluation Association. < *http://www.eval.org/publications/ GuidingPrinciplesPrintable.asp* >.

Behn, R. D. (2003). Eight purposes that public managers have for measuring performance. *Public Administration Review, 63*(5), 586-606.

Bickman, L., Rog, D. J., & Hedrick, T. E. (1998). Applied research design: A practical approach. In L. Bickman & D. J. Rog (Eds.), *Handbook of applied social research methods* (pp. 5-38). Thousand Oaks, CA: Sage.

Boruch, R. F. (1998). Randomized controlled experiments for evaluation and planning. In L. Bickman & D. J. Rog (Eds.), *Handbook of applied social research methods* (pp. 161-192). Thousand Oaks, CA: Sage.

Campbell, D. T. (1969). Reforms as experiments. *American Psychologist, 24*(4), 409-429.

Capowich, G. E., & Roehl, J. A. (1994). Problem-oriented policing: Actions and effectiveness in san diego. In D. Rosenbaum (Ed.), *The challenge of community policing: Testing the promises* (pp. 127-128). Thousand Oaks, CA: Sage.

Davidson, E. J. (2005). *Evaluation methodology basics: The nuts and bolts of sound evaluation*. Thousand Oaks, CA: Sage.

Eck, J. C., & Spelman, W. (1987). Who ya gonna call? the police as problem-busters. *Crime and Delinquency, 33*, 31-52.

Goldstein, H. (1979). Improving policing: A problem-oriented approach. *Crime and Delinquency, 25*, 236-258.

Goldstein, H. (1990). *Problem-oriented policing*. New York: McGraw Hill.

Inciardi, J. A., & Siegal, H. A. (1981). Whoring around: Some comments on deviance research in the private sector. *Criminology, 19*(2), 165-183.

Knowlton, L. W., & Phillips, C. (2013). *The logic model guidebook: Better strategies for great results* (2nd ed.). Thousand Oaks, CA: Sage.

Locke, E. A., & Latham, G. P. (2013). *New developments in goal setting and task performance*. East Sussex, UK: Routledge.

McDavid, J. C., & Hawthorn, L. R. (2006). *Program evaluation and performance management: An introduction to practice*. Thousand Oaks, CA: Sage.

Sieber, J. E. (1998). Planning ethically responsible research. In L. Bickman & D. J. Rog (Eds.), *Handbook of applied social research methods* (pp. 127-156). Thousand Oaks, CA: Sage.

Suchman, E. A. (1974). *Evaluative research: Principles and practice in public service and social action programs*. New York: Russell Sage Foundation.

Weiss, C. (1998). *Evaluation research: Methods for assessing program effectiveness*. Engelwood Cliffs, NJ: Prentice-Hall.

NEEDS ASSESSMENT EVALUATION

Keywords

community forums
focus groups
key informants
need quantitative data sources
qualitative data sources
social indicators

CHAPTER OUTLINE
Introduction   31
Definition of Needs   32
Data Sources   34
    Describing the Current Situation Can Occur in a Series of Steps   35
        Population Studied   35
        Assessing Current Resources   36
        Social Indicators   36
        Data Collection   37
    Surveys   38
    Treatment Groups   39
    Key Informants   39
    Focus Groups and Community Forums   40
        Analyze Data   42
        Needs Assessments and Program Planning   42
Problems with Needs Assessment   43
Summary   44
Discussion Questions   44
References   44

Introduction

Programs in criminal justice settings are developed to serve individuals who are in need and to create positive change. Governmental agencies and private funders provide funds to programs in schools, churches, towns, cities, prison institutions, and social service

agencies. This occurs because officials have determined that the needs of individuals involved with the criminal justice system have gone unmet. To determine what needs should be met, a few questions have to be addressed:
- How do officials determine that there is a need to be met?
- Who makes the determination?
- What information is necessary to demonstrate that a need exists?
- How should evaluators be used to assist in the planning of the proper types of programming?

The appearance of needs may seem media-driven. When the media reports a substantial number of homicides, robberies, or breaking and enterings, individuals in communities may not feel safe, even though they may not directly experience these types of acts (Alper & Chappell, 2012; Garofalo, 1981; Toet & van Shaik, 2012; Wallace, 2012). Further, some political-action groups or activist groups may seem to garner media attention that allows them to push their visions of needs (Alper & Chappell, 2012). While these uses of the media may provide some insight into genuine needs, officials usually require more quantified and qualified representative evidence. Thus, the term *needs* may mean different things for different individuals and groups.

In this chapter, we define needs so that the term resonates with evaluators to consistently check on how it is being used in a given situation. Then, along with their strengths and weaknesses, we present the methods that are commonly used to study needs for criminal justice. A solid evaluation begins in the planning stages of a program. The determination of needs is critical in the planning stages, but external evaluators are often not involved in this part of the process.

Definition of Needs

Needs may mean something different for a funder, government official, or evaluator—all of whom may be part of a program planning committee or evaluation. When this occurs, everyone involved may be working with a different set of assumptions. Worse yet, the term may not be defined at all. Without defining what is meant by needs, often evaluators and planners are referring to the discrepancy between what is and what should be (Rossi, Freeman, & Lipsey, 2004). Evaluators discuss many types of discrepancies that individuals may be referring too, but five states seem to be prevalent when needs are being discussed:
- Ideal.
- Norm.
- Minimum.
- Desired.
- Expected.

In a criminal justice setting, program planning committees or evaluators rarely discuss ideals. The discrepancy of norms may be discussed when criminals are not able to properly reintegrate into society. It is desirable for those who have drug problems to have access to rehabilitative facilities, or it is expected that they have this access. Scriven and Roth (1990) argued that individuals may not have a need when they are able to take part in an actual state that equals or exceeds the norm, minimum, desired, or expected state. This may lead to a faulty conclusion that a need is handled, taken care of, or that enough has been given. The definition of discrepancy, if used alone, provides an illogical focus, because many may not be aware that a program exists or are not able to meet the thresholds of the norm, minimum, desired, or expected state.

Evaluators will find it difficult to perform an evaluation without an explicit definition of needs. To obtain this explicit definition, it is imperative to work closely with planners and staff who may operate the program. In this book, we define a *need* as something that individuals must have to function satisfactorily within society. Without that "something" the individual will operate in an unsatisfactory state and possibly come into contact with the criminal justice system for the first time or as a recidivist; however, with that "something," the individual may operate satisfactorily in society. For instance, individuals who come to prison as drug addicts need access to a rehabilitation program, but access to a sexual addiction program may not be needed.

That assessment of the level of needs for planning or restructuring a criminal justice program could mean investigating potentially unavailable programs to individuals to a satisfactory state. Because criminal behavior transcends the criminal justice system to the individual and the community, the needs will be different for the criminal, the system, and the community. When breaking and entering into a residence occurs, the criminal who is caught for the offense will need a specific type of program. The victims of the breaking and entering may need different programs to work past the trauma of having their homes unlawfully entered. The community surrounding the residence may need a different program to prevent similar types of crimes from occurring again. At this point, one criminal act may create a need for several different types of programs.

Two problems arise when defining needs. One problem is determining the duration of a program. That is, whether individuals need something one time versus consistently over time. For instance, the victims of a breaking and entering may need a one-time program for financial assistance to repair damage to their home, but they may need consistent sessions with a therapist to overcome the trauma that comes from the event. Another problem is the scope of the need that results in the distribution of resources. Some individuals may not need a therapist to overcome victimization, but the community at large may need an available therapist for such an occasion.

Key features of estimating needs can help overcome some of these problems. Specifically, it is important to make sure that incidence and prevalence are addressed in the definition and determination of needs. *Incidence* refers to the number of individuals or groups experiencing a problem in a given time period. For instance, incidence of robbery may be high. This means that many people are robbed in a year. *Prevalence* refers to the number of individuals or groups who have the problem. For instance, the number of people who have been robbed may be high. These two features are critical to demonstrating needs because they provide some indication of the types of programming that may be necessary and the distribution of resources. A program that addresses a problem that is widespread and temporary may not need the same types of resources as a problem that is less widespread but longer lasting. For example, attempts to help drug users overcome their addictions (i.e., less widespread but longer lasting) are different than attempts to help parolees gain employable skills (i.e., widespread but temporary), but keep in mind there are sizeable numbers of each.

Needs do not have to be defined in a way such that everyone is aware that they are deficient. Individuals or groups may be unaware that they have a need (e.g., outdated job skills), they deny a need (e.g., drug addicts usually resist or deny the need for rehabilitation), or they misidentify a need (e.g., juveniles committing delinquency so that they may be accepted in delinquent social networks). Most of the time, individuals and groups are acutely aware that they have a need, but often their view is tainted by self-interest or a myopic focus.

Due to the self-interest or myopic focus of individuals or groups, a needs assessment evaluation may be necessary. A *needs assessment evaluation* refers to the systematic process to acquire an accurate, thorough picture of issues or needs that may arise in a criminal justice setting (e.g., community or organization). By including multiple data sources and stakeholders, this type of evaluation provides the basic framework for the planning and development of services or programming to alleviate various needs.

Data Sources

The data sources that are necessary to address a problem are quantitative and qualitative data. These data sources should provide a clear picture of the social and economic conditions of all parts of the criminal justice system that are involved or affected by a program.

Table 3.1 Steps in the Needs Assessment Process

Step	Parts of Needs Assessment
1	Identify the population being studied
2	Examine existing resources
3	Consult social indicators
4	Determine how needs assessment data will be collected
5	Analysis of data
6	Use the results for planning

This would include facts and opinions of community residents, criminal justice practitioners (e.g., law enforcement, court workers, and corrections), and criminals. While it appears that a solid assessment of needs includes information from individuals from all of these groups, it is wise to think about how each individual's unmet needs are being studied, and what resources are available to them. This has to occur, because performing a needs assessment is not always straightforward. An evaluator may not have a complete understanding of the environment where a need is present. To assist the evaluator in performing a needs assessment, the next section consists of a series of steps to perform a needs assessment. Table 3.1 shows all of the steps in the project.

Describing the Current Situation Can Occur in a Series of Steps

Population Studied

The first step is to identify the population that is being studied. It might be a school district, correctional facility, law enforcement agency, or courtroom. Rather than define the population as everyone in a geographically defined area, the evaluator has to narrow his or her definition of a population to things like gang-involved juveniles, unemployed parolees, police districts with high homicide rates, or courtrooms with inefficient court dockets. Further, describing the population's size, characteristics, and location would be relevant before beginning.

When dealing with governmental criminal justice agencies, evaluators may rely on legally defined limits of authority and responsibility to help in the narrowing process. When dealing with private agencies that provide social services in conjunction with criminal justice agencies (e.g., clinical social workers, hospitals, or nonprofit organizations), the narrowing process may become difficult because these agencies do not have legal limits of responsibility, but they may desire to assist a large group of individuals. For instance, a proposed private community corrections facility would want to know how many of its potential clients or potential employers for their clients are in the area. Some of this information would be easy to obtain; other information (e.g., community resistance) may be hard and costly to obtain. The needs assessment report shows that part of the relevant group has unmet needs, and that other subgroups do not require additional attention.

At this point, an evaluator has importance. He or she may be able to talk about juvenile delinquency, for example, and relate the percentage of juveniles between 13 and 17 years old who are arrested each year for a given area. This allows the evaluator to positively contribute to the planning and evaluation of a program.

Assessing Current Resources

The second step is to examine the existing resources. Needs assessments are often criticized because they tend to place a substantial amount of emphasis on the problems that have to be addressed with very little or any assessment of existing resources. In other words, without knowing what resources are present, exist, or could be strengthened could result in wasting or duplicating resources. For instance, say a school houses a gang-resistance program. Without knowing this information, planners and evaluators may attempt to add a different gang-resistance program in the same school. Thus, evaluators have to include a catalog of the current programs and supports (i.e., churches, schools, employers, etc.) for a needs assessment. Using this information is an important foundation and collaboration that can provide something that individuals must have to function satisfactorily within society.

Social Indicators

The third step is to consult social indicators. Social indicators show changes in conditions that provide some insight that a problem or need exists. Tracking official records of crime, delinquency, unemployment of parolees, recidivism, or school dropout rates may provide some indication of the types of problems that could influence criminal justice. Increases in these types of social indicators suggest a need for a program, but when these problems are addressed properly through careful planning and programming, they will be lower.

Social indicators may be found in several different places. The decennial federal census provides a way to measure the extent of needs using social indicators. The census is divided into census tracts, which allow the evaluator to obtain information about a given community. This type of summary data may provide information that could indicate unmet needs. Since the census is stratified by race, gender, and age, it is possible to further narrow areas of need. Evaluators are able to use entire regions, states, or the nation to make it easier to detect differences that reveal needs.

In criminal justice, social indicators may come from several different places, including the Federal Bureau of Investigation, Office of Juvenile Justice and Delinquency Prevention, and Federal Bureau of Prisons. Evaluators may supplement these social indicators with figures that come from the Department of Health and Human Services, Center for Disease Control, or National Institute of Drug Abuse and National Institute of Mental Health. Social indicators for criminal justice are plentiful, and they do not always have to come as official statistics like those from these sources. Evaluators may use social indicator information from peer-reviewed articles or reports about the topic of interest. Evaluators with some experience are able to use social indicators without incurring much expense beyond time and effort for a quality needs assessment.

Using social indicators to identify a problem and shape programs requires knowledge of the indirect measurement and context of the problem. This simply means that the evaluator has to be knowledgeable about the issue in general. This knowledge provides suggestions of the proper types of programs that are necessary to reduce instances of the problem or alleviate the need, bringing about the satisfactory state. For example, even if everyone agreed on the different reasons underlying a problem, if a psychologist is not performing well in group sessions in the rehabilitation program, perhaps higher salaries are necessary to attract better psychologists.

An important issue arises with social indicators—they have limits. Many social indicators do not capture every instance of a behavior or action; in some instances, some behaviors or actions that did not occur will be included; and in some instances, some behaviors or actions may be misclassified by those in charge of reporting social indicators. With these limits, some believe that social indicators are not to be used in needs assessments. This is not a valid stance, because social indicators provide some indication of the incidence and prevalence of a problem. Other sources of information can assist evaluators and planners to be more specific about the causes of the underlying problems and the different options to alleviate them.

Data Collection

The fourth step is to determine how the needs assessment data will be collected. The evaluator has to make some decisions about the use of surveys, treatment groups, and key informants. Resources will play an important role in these decisions. Surveys may be expensive given the population. Using key informants may be impossible to perform. The evaluator has to determine which ways of conducting the needs assessment will provide the best information.

Surveys

A straightforward way to estimate individuals' needs is to ask them. Individuals are keen on expressing their opinions on the development of criminal justice services or programs. The opinion of individuals may be helpful in the planning stages. Choosing this type of methodology may be helpful in determining the groups that may receive the survey. For instance, if a program intends to help burglars, the group to survey is those who are burglars. The evaluator is likely to violate a major assumption of methodology and statistics—representativeness. *Representativeness* refers to everyone in the identified population having an equal and known opportunity to be part of the survey. This is not likely to happen because of the enormity of the population and not all burglars are known. Thus, the evaluator has to rely on the professionals in the criminal justice system to provide names, or ask the burglars to provide additional names.

Survey preparation requires a specialized skill set. The discussion of survey writing is addressed fully in Chapter 8. Here, the presentation is general and brief. Writing clear and concise questions for a survey is as much art as it is skill. The questions have to be direct without leading the respondent, and depend on the topic being studied. The writing involved in the questions has to provide a sense of simplicity so that the respondent is not overwhelmed by each item. Essential to the survey is to provide information about incidence and prevalence while capturing information about the potentially different approaches. Survey writers could easily write items or questions that could make endorsing some plans easy. For instance, if the individual responding to the survey (i.e., respondent) is asked to mark all services listed that should be present in his or her neighborhood. This type of questioning gets to the apex of the matter, but it has flaws for several reasons:

- The question is only about solutions and not about the problem.
- The question is leading.
- The question does not discuss the potential cost of providing services or that providing these services means that other services cannot be provided.

These three issues will make substantial differences in endorsement.

Depending on the administration (i.e., door-to-door, institution-to-institution, over the phone, online surveys, or face-to-face), surveys may be a drain on resources. For instance, administering a survey where it is face-to-face or door-to-door may put the survey administrator's safety at risk. Over the phone surveys are expensive, and, with the advent of the mobile phone, phone surveys are much more difficult to administer, not to mention expensive. Mailing a survey is expensive and could produce few responses. Online surveys may be helpful because they are relatively inexpensive and only require an Internet connection, computer, and email.

Treatment Groups

Individuals with a specific need will seek out a program to alleviate the need (a.k.a. treatment group). An evaluator may contrast the extent of a need by estimating the level of services currently available throughout the criminal justice system or community. As mentioned before, a thorough cataloging of services is imperative to make sure that duplication is not occurring. For instance, planners proposing to develop a drug rehabilitation center in an urban area need to list the proximity, treatment types, and capacity for clients of other drug rehabilitation centers in the area.

When this is not possible, planners may be able to better understand the treatment group by using agency files. The agency files provide demographic information to better understand potential clients. Keep in mind that all individuals may not be part of the treatment group, and this occurs for several reasons, such as they are not qualified or cannot afford the cost. When individuals qualify for the treatment group, the presentation of the demographic information must always protect the confidentiality of the potential clients. When seeking these files, it is instructive to ask the agency for additional leads to those providing these services. This is important, because informal programs may be operating as well, making exact or relative amounts of individuals using these services difficult to ascertain.

Key Informants

Key informants are individuals who know the criminal justice system or their part of the criminal justice system and may know what needs are going unmet. Locating key informants is not a small or easy task. To begin identifying these individuals, start with those who have the task of bringing individuals into contact with those with a mutually agreed-upon need. Within the criminal justice system, begin with probation or parole officers, law enforcement officers, judges, or social workers. Outside the criminal justice system, begin with clergy, politicians, or YMCA leaders. Individuals in these groups are likely to have some recommendations for programming.

These individuals are important because they have the closest contact with the individuals in need. While this is an important useful step, this may also be a detriment. Those who are so close to individuals in need will have a tendency to project their need onto others, resulting in an overestimation of need. This is not the fault of the key informant because the individual in need has made such an impression that he or she is memorable. The desire to help the situation usually begins to cloud the key informant's estimation of the true need. The evaluator needs to maintain objectivity and begin a thorough investigation of the need and recommended programming.

Key informants tend to be experts in their areas because of education, training, or experience. While this is wonderful for initial discovery of problems and needs, their expertise tends to force them into single-minded focus of a problem or need. This single-minded focus tends to be at odds with other experts familiar with the same problem or need.

An example of the results of such differences was provided by a YMCA director who consistently hears from teachers that they want to improve the behavior of young boys. The YMCA director reasoned:

1. Young boys usually do not behave well and other YMCA directors agree that behavioral improvement is desirable.
2. YMCA directors and staff have only limited contact with the young boys compared to parents or teachers.
3. Therefore, one way to improve the behavior of young boys is help teachers better understand how to monitor the boys in school.

The YMCA director developed a series of workshops for the teachers, obtained support from the school district, and acquired a limited amount of funds from the Parent Teacher Association for a guest speaker. The problems with the YMCA director's plan are elementary. The YMCA director assumes that the teachers' complaints are actually commitments to improvement. Although the teachers complain about the young boys' behavior, few are apt to involve themselves in the process of correcting the problem. Consequently, few teachers attended the first workshop, and those who do attend say that they have little problem with young boys' behavior. Further workshops do not take place.

The YMCA director seems to focus on one solution too quickly without paying particular attention to how others may react to the plan. When focusing on one particular plan, the ability to make cogent arguments for other plans shows that sticking to one plan may overestimate the likelihood of success. When measuring the need and considering alternative approaches, it is important to explore a myriad of ideas.

Focus Groups and Community Forums

Rather than performing surveys, evaluators are able to use other methods to collect valuable information. These methods provide opportunities for criminal justice practitioners or criminals to express their views about their needs. Evaluators may use two approaches to collect these data: focus groups and community forums.

Focus groups are an important technique to gather information. Market research firms consistently use focus group research to address important issues (e.g., products, ideas for new products, packaging, and purchasing). Focus group participants address open-ended questions in interviews. A focus group is a small, informal group of individuals (usually 7–10 members) from the target or potential treatment group. A leader of a focus group tries to stay out of the way to foster a relaxed atmosphere and the sharing of opinions among members. The focus group leader keeps everyone on topic. The focus group should consist of individuals who possess similar demographics. The goal is free sharing of opinions, but the group members may differ. This has the potential to limit participation. Regardless of similarities in demographics, the individuals do not usually know one another, and they are not likely to see one another after the focus group. Some financial incentive is usually given for participation in the focus group to cover travel and two hours of discussion.

Focus groups are relevant at any part of a needs evaluation. Focus groups are powerful in understanding the reactions to potential programs or changes in programs. While individuals may not know all of the details of a new program, their views are important to take into consideration in the development of a program. One use of focus groups is to provide an in-depth understanding of survey results. A survey may say that a drug rehabilitation program needs some changes. Once important plans are put into place to change the drug rehabilitation program, focus groups of potential treatment groups and staff may provide powerful reactions to the plan, especially if the questions are open-ended.

A community forum is another method of capturing group interactions. Community forums differ in how the individuals are selected to participate. In focus groups, demographics are the thrust behind the decision to include an individual. Community forums are a self-selected group. When programs or policies on a large scale are up for consideration, agencies—government or private—may announce the date and time of a community meeting to consider some planning issue. Only the individuals who hear of the meeting and choose to participate may attend. In this format, the evaluator should divide large groups into smaller groups. Using open-ended questions, the smaller groups address the issues. The needs of the groups are identified and should be ranked.

Community forums have an advantage and a few disadvantages. Evaluators using community forums are able to gather information from individuals at a low cost, and they provide an environment for the possibility of good ideas. One disadvantage is that the groups are self-selected, which means that the groups may not be representative of the larger group. These are individuals who heard about and are motivated enough to attend this type of meeting. Another disadvantage is that community forums raise expectations that something can and will be done to meet the needs being discussed. An additional disadvantage is that assertive individuals may turn the community forum into a gripe session without producing information about the needs of the community.

Analyze Data

The fifth step of the needs assessment is the analysis of the data. For the parts of the needs assessment that are quantitative, statistical analysis may be necessary. Statistical analysis is covered in Chapter 8. For the parts of the needs assessment that use qualitative data, the evaluator needs to draw out important and relevant themes. Themes are thought, word, or sentiment expressed consistently across groups. In combination with statistical analysis, the themes from the qualitative data provide a complete context of the needs for an organization.

Needs Assessments and Program Planning

The sixth step is using the results for planning. After assessing the level of need for the criminal justice population of interest, then program planning may take place. The planners develop a service or program to help the population achieve or approach a satisfactory state. For instance, an assessment may show that a community needs an after-school program to reduce instances of juvenile loitering after school hours in the general public areas. The success of the service or program improves when key stakeholders are included in the program development process. The success of the after-school program requires the inclusion and commitment of the school system, other service providers such as the YMCA, and parents. The formal stakeholders may be involved through formal representation on committees or through focus groups to develop plans. The plans have to include outcome goals. Discussions with the community school system and YMCA reveal that the outcome goal is to reduce juvenile loitering by 25%.

Once the outcome goals have been specified from the needs assessment, the next step is to consider the intermediate goals that need to be achieved to reach the outcome goals. The intermediate goals may be an increase in knowledge, skills, accomplishments, behaviors, or attitudes. Keeping with the after-school program example, the intermediate goals of physical fitness and intense homework assistance help the juveniles improve their health and grades. While the juveniles are participating in these activities in the after-school program, they are not loitering as much. Planners, however, have to take care to explicate the program theory. In other words, the planners have to be careful to ask what has to happen to the program participants before they can reach the outcomes. With the juvenile after-school program, the theory is to keep the juveniles involved in academic and health-related activities so they will be less likely to loiter. When this occurs, the planners are developing the impact model as the program is being planned.

Once the impact model is developed, the planners are able to specify the actions necessary to implement the program. The resources that are necessary to be considered are paramount. For the after-school program, the planners have the following needs (obviously these are large categories with smaller needs embedded in them): knowledgeable staff, infrastructure to house the program, financial resources to pay for the program, and advertising materials. The planners have to work with each of the needs against one another. For instance, the need for knowledgeable staff is balanced with financial resources, and the same goes for the other needs. When the planners are not able to balance the financial resources against the needs of the program, the planners have to make decisions. For instance, if the financial resources show that the number of knowledgeable staff for the after-school program is low, the planners have to make a decision as to whether they are going to reduce services or the number of juveniles to be served.

The process that has been described here may seem linear or straightforward. In reality, the planners will work back and forth from the goals to the sponsoring organization's mission. Sometimes planners will discover that some intermediate goals may be unrealistic. Consider an intermediate goal of the after-school program is improving weight loss among the juveniles participating. While some weight loss may occur for some, it is unrealistic to assume the weight loss will occur for all who need it. The planners may have to go back and rethink or drop the intermediate goal of weight loss. Properly designed programs work in a backward fashion. The outcome goals are clear and established first, and the steps to achieve the goal occur afterwards.

Problems with Needs Assessment

A needs assessment is important because it improves the quality of program planning. Planners or evaluators are not able to develop a comprehensive set of program objectives when the needs of the program are not explicitly known. This means that the program may operate inefficiently or ineffectively, which is not a good way to use scarce resources. Needs assessments may not always provide the most comprehensive information. Many needs assessments do not fully consider the needs of the intended individuals. This is to say that program planners and evaluators may create a program that does not meet the desired needs. Further, many programs do not seem to take the context of the program into account. Many programs do not consider the following: a community, correctional institution, or law enforcement may not have the capacity to handle the program. With all of this information in mind, planning a program may begin.

Summary

The importance of assessing needs before beginning to plan programs cannot be overstated. Needs are nothing more than what is necessary for an individual to be in a satisfactory state. Needs are not what the individual would like to have. Needs are not fully understood, and this makes it necessary to gather substantial amounts of information through surveys, social indicators, and focus group information. Once the needs are clear, it is important to begin planning.

Discussion Questions

1. Why it is difficult to explicate the definition of needs?
2. How do evaluators use needs assessments in planning programs?
3. Describe the difference between treatment groups and community forums.
4. Describe how a needs assessment could be threatening to a criminal justice organization.
5. Many criminal justice agencies strive to rehabilitate individuals from their criminal behavior. Sketch a plan to do an assessment of the needs for such a program. Consider the information that you want and the sources, as well as the methodology to use in gathering the necessary information.

References

Alper, M., & Chappell, A. T. (2012). Untangling fear of crime: A multi-theoretical approach to examining the causes of crime-specific fear. *Sociological Spectrum, 32*(4), 346–363.

Garofalo, J. (1981). Fear of crime: Causes and consequences. *Journal of Criminology and Criminal Law, 72*, 839.

Rossi, P. H., Freeman, H. W., & Lipsey, M. W. (2004). *Evaluation: A systematic approach* (7th ed.). Thousand Oaks, CA: Sage.

Scriven, M., & Roth, J. (1990). Special feature: Needs assessment. *Evaluation Review, 11*, 135–140.

Toet, A., & van Schaik, M. G. (2012). Effects of signals of disorder on fear of crime in real and virtual environments. *Journal of Environmental Psychology, 32*(3), 260–276.

Wallace, D. (2012). Examining fear and stress as mediators between disorder perceptions and personal health, depression, and anxiety. *Social Science Research, 41*(6), 1515–1528.

THEORY-DRIVEN EVALUATION

Keywords

evaluability assessment approach
program impact theory
service utilization plan
organizational plan

CHAPTER OUTLINE
Introduction 47
Evaluability Assessment Approach 49
Describing and Producing Program Theory 50
    Program Impact Theory   52
    Service Utilization Plan   53
    Program Organizational Plan   53
        Step 1: Define Boundaries   *54*
        Step 2: Explicate Program Theory   *55*
        Step 3: Define Program Goals and Objectives   *55*
        Step 4: Describe the Program Functions, Components, and Activities   *56*
        Step 5: Final Corroboration of the Description of the Program Theory   *56*
Analyzing Program Theory 57
    Link between Program Theory and Social Needs   58
    Evaluating Logic and Plausibility of Program Theory   59
    Comparing Research with Practice   60
Summary 61
Discussion Questions 61
References 61

Introduction

In this chapter, we focus on the concepts and procedures necessary for a criminal justice program evaluator to examine the conceptualization of a program, also known as *program theory*. Program theory may be expressed implicitly or explicitly. Either way, it explains why a program does what it does and provides the rationale that doing so will achieve the expected or desired results. At the outset of evaluating program theory, criminal justice evaluators may be dismayed by the incomplete or nonexistence of program theory. Many criminal justice programs are poorly designed with errors that can be traced back to a program's conceptualization. These errors are the result of neglecting the objectives and theory in the planning stages, or implementation, discussed in Chapter 3. This is not always the fault of program planners. Sometimes the political climate surrounding criminal justice programs does not allow for extensive planning. Unfortunately, when this is not the case, the conceptualization of the program theory gets little attention.

In criminal justice, this may be the case. Many times, programs are borne from familiar or "off-the-shelf" services without a clear understanding of the match between the program and services (Coryn, Noakes, Westine & Schroter, 2011). In other words, the match between the program and services and needs is not clear. For instance, crime programs generally have a mix of education and counseling. The unfortunate issue is that the underlying assumptions—individuals will change their behavior due to education or counseling—are not discussed or made explicit. Evidence has shown that criminal behavior is often resistant to change from education or counseling. Therefore, using only this as an underlying set of assumptions may not produce the desired results.

The rationale of a program and conceptualization deserves a substantial amount of scrutiny in an evaluation. The scrutiny should result in an understanding of the criminal justice program's goals and objectives. Welsh (2006) argues that program objectives must be clearly specified and, optimally, be measurable. However, if these goals and objectives do not match the needs that the program is designed to improve, at best, the program can only be expected to be marginally effective (Welsh & Harris, 2004).

A necessary function in assessing the program theory is to articulate it—that is, make sure that the descriptions of concepts (i.e., abstractions from reality), assumptions (i.e., hypotheses), and expectations (i.e., ideas for outcomes) are in congruence with the manner in which the program is structured and operated. It is a rare case that a criminal justice program will reveal its theory to an evaluator. While implicit, this occurs because the entire statement of the program theory is rarely written down. For instance, a program designed to prevent juveniles from joining gangs called Gang Resistance Education and Training (GREAT) has a nine-lesson curriculum that is delivered to middle-school children. Esbensen & Osgood (1999) argue that the curriculum was not developed with any specific theory in mind, but they state that curriculum does have its basic etiology from criminological theory. Even when it is written, the explication of the program theory comes from an abstract grant or funding proposal that has not been consulted during implementation or program practice.

Criminal justice program evaluators have an important task to understand and clearly delineate the program theory in a manner that can be used for an evaluation. This chapter will use two views as guides to help criminal justice program evaluators understand and clearly delineate program theory. First is presenting program theory in a way that represents stakeholders' views and understanding of the program that makes it workable for a program evaluation through the evaluability assessment approach. Second is describing a program theory for different parts of a program.

Evaluability Assessment Approach

The first approach is a presentation of an evaluability assessment. An *evaluability assessment* refers to a method of identifying and describing the program theory by outlining its components and deciphering which of them is measurable (Welsh, 2006). Van Voorhis, Cullen & Applegate (1995) argue that evaluability assessments are designed to ascertain if a program has a sound theoretical basis, has a well-designed treatment protocol, has been implemented as designed, and is suitable for further inquiry such as an outcome evaluation.

This type of assessment is important for several reasons. First, the program theory may or may not be clear. Second, the program staff may or may not have differing views about the program theory. Understanding the program theory and the views of the program's staff are important for the evaluator. Knowing this information, the evaluator is able to sort out with the stakeholder the program theory that can be used to evaluate the program.

Performing an evaluability assessment can take many forms. Van Voorhis & Brown (1996) argue that an evaluability assessment requires four steps:

1. Identify the purpose and scope of the assessment.
2. Develop a program template that describes the goals and objectives of the program, the theory underlying the program, and the intended treatment protocol.
3. Validate the program design through interviews and focus groups with program staff members and stakeholders and through observations of program activities.
4. Prepare a report that details the assessment findings and provides the proper recommendations for future evaluation or program improvements.

Welsh (2006) takes a different focus in outlining the process for an evaluability assessment. He argues that the evaluator should do the following:

1. Review the documentation that describes the program.
2. Interview administrators and line staff members.

3. Read case files.
4. Interview program staff.

The evaluability assessment may provide information to improve the program. Smith (1989) argues that evaluability assessments generally show the problems within a program, including:
- The need to clarify the target population.
- The need to reconceptualize the intervention.
- The realization that few objectives are agreed upon by stakeholders and program staff.

The evaluability assessment can make it clear that more work is necessary to fine tune the program. Welsh (2006) argues that this type of assessment results in a program model that can be reviewed by program administrators and staff for accuracy. Regardless, if the intent is to arrive at information from Smith's (1989) perspective or Welsh's (2006) perspective, the evaluability assessment may help program staff deal with differences.

While this type of evaluation may be used for a single program, Matthews, Hubbard & Latessa (2001) see evaluability assessment as a means of improving correctional programming on a large scale. Using the Correctional Program Assessment Inventory (CAPI), Matthews et al. (2001) examine whether 86 treatment programs are meeting the principles of effective intervention. The results of this assessment show that 34.1% of the programs studied were unsatisfactorily meeting the principles of effective intervention. The main problem with these programs is that they lack integrity. In other words, the evaluability assessment shows that the programs are not being implemented properly. While this perspective is good for improvements, it does not necessarily focus on a description of the program theory. This perspective, rather, uses the program theory as part of the evaluability assessment to determine the problems with the program. In other words, the program theory may be lost using this model. An evaluability assessment may be fruitful for eliciting program theory on a program-by-program basis.

Describing and Producing Program Theory

The second approach is describing and producing program theory because not all evaluations involve the entire program theory. Each part of the program may operate using different theories. This approach focuses on describing program theory for different parts of the program rather than the entire program.

The evaluation literature has long recognized the importance of program theory and its potential uses for formulating and prioritizing questions, research designs, and interpreting evaluation findings

(Chen, 2005; Chen & Rossi, 1980, 1983). Chen (1990) writes that program theory is important because not using this type of theory results in an evaluation that is mechanical or uniform without concern for the theoretical implications of the program's content, setting, participants, or implementing organizations. In other words, without using program theory, the evaluation is only able to determine if the program met narrowly defined goals rather than satisfied theoretical implications. Chen (1990) notes:

> *The question is of whether or not goals are appropriate for the effectiveness of the program, or whether these rational goals and procedures could lead to unintended consequences, might not be considered. Evaluators may sometimes be serving only bureaucratic interests and neglect the broader implications for human needs and purposes from the perspective of the stakeholders. To avoid such problems, a new conceptual framework for evaluation should be concerned with value rationality and should provide more insight into the real purposes of a program and its implication for wider social interests. (p. 34)*

In criminal justice, evaluations do happen in this manner. For instance, the early evaluations of boot camps as shock incarceration fall into this category. Four- to six-month boot camp–like situations that emphasize military-style discipline and physical exercise served as a correctional alternative to incarceration in the 1990s. The early evaluations of this type of program only considered the goals (i.e., reduce recidivism) (MacKenzie & Shaw, 1993) and not the broader theoretical implications (i.e., get tough on crime or self-regulation through self-esteem improvement).

With this in mind, we take the perspective that a program involves a series of interactions between the program staff and target population. These interactions may involve a multitude of things (e.g., counseling sessions, education sessions, nutrition, medical services, etc.). There are multiple interactions in a program. For instance, the program serves as the organization (i.e., infrastructure, personnel, resources, or activities), and the target population brings their lives (i.e., circumstances) to the organization. These factors may influence the success of the program.

This perspective brings three components together: impact theory, service utilization plan, and the program's organizational plan (Rossi, Lipsey & Freeman, 2004). The impact theory provides instances about the change process and the change in the conditions. Central to the impact theory is the program's staff–target population interactions because this is the only way that the change can occur. The impact theory may be simple, complex, formal, or informal, but the end result is that change occurred. If change did not occur, then something is faulty about the impact theory.

The impact of a program does not occur by itself. Programs need a stimulus to provide services to the target population. To provide the services as sufficiently as possible, program staff turn to the service utilization plan. The service utilization plan is vital to a theory-driven evaluation because it contains the assumptions and expectations for reaching the target population. In other words, the service utilization plan provides the proper manner to initiate and terminate the service.

The program has to be developed and organized in a manner to provide the intended services. The organizational plan provides a schematic as to how the program resources, personnel, administration, and general organization are composed and utilized. The organizational plan is a series of hypotheses that tie together the infrastructure, personnel, resources, etc. to provide the services as intended. The combination of resources and organization come together so that the service may be provided and maintained. The organization and services are under the control of program staff. These two things—organization and service—represent the program's process.

Program Impact Theory

Program impact theory is about causality. This type of theory describes the cause-and-effect sequence of events that come from the program. Specifically, there is a stimulus and certain outcomes that come from the stimulus. Generally, evaluators discuss program impact theory using a causal diagram that outlines the cause-and-effect events (Chen, 1990). However, it is relevant for an evaluator to keep in mind that programs rarely have direct control over the social conditions that they are expected to improve, and this means that they will have some indirect effect for a benefit to occur.

The most basic form of program impact theory takes place in two stages. In the first stage the services are administered that influence some intermediate condition, and in the second stage some improvement occurs (Chen, 2011). For example, a program to improve alcohol abuse will use motivation or attitudinal services to influence the intermediate conditions that lead to alcohol abuse. While this type of theoretical premise is worthwhile, many programs operate in a more complex manner. The complexity comes with many more stages between the program and the benefits, and this may or may not mean more than one path to the benefit.

The key to representing any program impact theory is that each part of the program will have a cause-and-effect feature. That is, each service will cause a linkage between some other services within the program. In the boot camp example, the impact theory is that discipline, exercise, and education will result in less recidivism because the attendees have better levels of self-regulation.

Service Utilization Plan

The service utilization plan provides a clear understanding of how and why program participants became or will become involved in the program. This plan continues to show how the participant will follow through to the point of completing the program. In other words, the service utilization plan provides an outline of program-targets interactions from the perspective of the participant, and his or her journey through the program. For instance, a drug treatment program will have a specific plan as to how counselors and attendees will interact. The plan may consist of days, times, locations, and types of materials.

Program Organizational Plan

As the service utilization plan is written from the perspective of the participant, the program organizational plan is written from the perspective of program management. This plan brings together the functions and activities of the program. Further, the program organizational plan provides management with the expectations of the program and the resources (i.e., human, financial, and infrastructure) that are required for the program to function. Key to this plan is the program services that the management or staff are to perform so that the participants are able to reap the intended benefits. The program organizational plan has to provide information about the sustainability of the program, including fundraising, personnel management, facilities acquisition and maintenance, and political climate.

A program's organizational plan may be shown in several different ways. Focusing on the interactions between the program and its participants allows the first element—a description of the program's objectives for the services provided—of the program organizational plan to permeate to the top. If this element does not permeate to the top, a number of questions may assist in this process:
- What are the services?
- How much is to be provided?
- To whom are the services to be provided?
- On what schedule are the services to be provided?

The second element of the program organizational plan is to describe the resources and functions that are necessary for the program. This includes a description of the personnel with proper credentials and skills, logistics, proper facilities, funding, supervision, or clerical support.

Having been exposed to the issues noted here does not guarantee that it is clear on how to extract program theory. The production of program theory is important to develop a high-quality program evaluation. Program theory may be articulated or spelled out clearly so that everyone understands the theory behind the program. This tends to occur when a program comes from a criminological theory. For instance, social learning theory may be a theoretical premise used to reduce instances of gang involvement.

Unfortunately, all program theory is not well articulated. This is known as implicit program theory (Chen, 1990). This type of theory means the underlying assumptions about program services and practices are not well discussed and articulated, in the context of theory. This type of program theory provides evaluators the most trouble.

Implicit program theory requires the evaluator to extract and describe the theory before it can be analyzed or evaluated. The evaluator has to determine the intentions of the program framers and stakeholders about what the program should be doing. The extraction of this type of theory works best using a set of steps.

Step 1: Define Boundaries

The first step of extracting an implicit program theory is defining the boundaries of the program, which are contingent on the scope of the program and the scope of the program staff's concerns. An evaluator may identify the boundaries of the program if he or she works from the perspective of the decision makers. The decision makers should have some idea of the activities of the program and organizational structures. In other words, the decision makers, especially those who are charged with acting on the results of the evaluation, should have some idea where the other decision makers stand on the reasons why the program exists and how the program should operate.

The definition of program boundaries has to include all the important activities, events, or resources that have a link with one or more outcomes that are central to the program. The evaluator may be able to uncover these boundaries by beginning with the benefit from the program and working backward to identify the relevant activities and resources that may make a contribution to organizational or programmatic objectives. From this perspective, a drug treatment program at the local or state level could be distilled as a set of activities that are organized by a rehabilitation group to alleviate drug abuse in a specified participant group.

While these two approaches are good starting points, their rational presentation may oversimplify the process of extracting program theory. Evaluators have to keep in mind that programs may be complex. Further, each of the objectives of a program may be difficult to establish. This puts the evaluator into a position where he or she has to negotiate the definition of program boundaries with program staff, stakeholders, and decision makers. Further, evaluators have to recognize that the definition of boundaries is a fluid process that requires them to be flexible.

For example, Esbensen & Osgood (1999) describe the boundaries of the GREAT program. The program is designed to reduce instances of juveniles joining gangs. To address this specific need, the GREAT program is bound to middle-school students, and the curriculum is delivered by law enforcement. Here, the boundaries are the age group (i.e., 11–13 year olds) of the students.

Step 2: Explicate Program Theory

Not all program theory is original. Some program theory may come from prior experience of program planners, research, or practice. This is a welcomed situation for an evaluator because he or she is able to develop a well-articulated theory. The evaluator encounters issues when dealing with an existing program. He or she has to work through the structure and operations of the program to derive the theory. This means that the evaluator has to work with stakeholders to bring out the theory that comes from their actions and assumptions. The evaluator accomplishes this by producing multiple drafts describing the program theory. He or she presents these drafts to stakeholders and decision makers to ensure that their approximations of the program theory are correct.

Esbensen & Osgood (1999) describe the development of the GREAT program in this manner. In 1991, when the Phoenix, AZ, Police Department introduced GREAT as a school-based program, they used D.A.R.E. (Drug Abuse Resistance Education) as a model to create a nine-week curriculum. D.A.R.E. is a program specifically designed to provide resistance training and education for drug use. This program generally consists of a 17-lesson curriculum that is offered once a week in schools. Both curriculums for GREAT and D.A.R.E. are offered by trained law enforcement officers.

To begin the process of drafting a program theory like this one, the evaluator needs to turn to several sources for information. The evaluator has to analyze the program documents. This can be all reports, mission statements, or goal statements. Then, the evaluator should interview the stakeholders and decision makers. This will provide information from both of these respective sides of the program. Next, the evaluator should perform site visits to observe the functions and circumstances of which the program operates in its natural environment. Finally, the evaluator should consult the criminological literature. Information from these places will assist the evaluator in drafting a reasonable program theory, but the final verdict comes from the review of the program theory by the stakeholders and decision makers.

Step 3: Define Program Goals and Objectives

Program goals and objectives are central to program theory. They provide an understanding of what the program should be accomplishing. The issue that often arises with program goals and objectives is that they do not also mesh with mission statements, or they may not mesh with the responses or needs of stakeholders. This means that the evaluator has to be able to explicate the program goals and objectives that are realistic to the outcomes of the program. An important issue that the evaluator has to keep in mind is the consistency between the actual accomplishments of the program and the intended accomplishments of the program. This means that the evaluator should review the major program activities as well as the written goals of the program.

This definition of goals becomes part of the program theory; however, the goals and objectives have to be properly placed in the program theory. For instance, goals and objectives that bring about change are impact theory, but goals and objectives concerning program activities are service delivery. If the program aims to reduce juvenile delinquency, this is part of the impact theory, but if the aim is to offer after-school care for juveniles to reduce unstructured socialization, then a portion of the service delivery plan is present.

An example of this process is the GREAT program. Esbensen & Osgood (1999) argue that the objective of the program is to reduce gang activity and educate juveniles about the consequences of gang involvement. In a broader sense, GREAT provides life skills that empower juveniles with the ability to resist joining gangs through cognitive behavioral strategies.

Step 4: Describe the Program Functions, Components, and Activities

An evaluator has to be able to properly describe all of the program functions, components, and activities. Program functions include everything that a program does (e.g., intake, recruitment, etc.). These types of activities are central to the understanding of the program theory. Without them, the description of the program theory will be incomplete.

The evaluator must also be able to link the program functions, components, and activities into a logical sequence of events that occurs within the program. This is consistent with the development of a logic model. In the GREAT program, the law enforcement officers who come to the school to deliver the curriculum engage the juveniles in instruction, discussion, and role-playing. These activities provide the opportunity to introduce conflict resolution skills, cultural sensitivity skills, and the negative aspects of gang life (Esbensen & Osgood, 1999).

Step 5: Final Corroboration of the Description of the Program Theory

The evaluator has to keep in mind that the result of these steps will be a program theory that is consistent with what the program was intended to do rather than the actual state of the program. This occurs because those involved think in ideal terms rather than real terms. In other words, those involved with the program tend to focus on alleviating a social problem, and do not see the faults of the program. The program staff who are further away from the program will see it in a manner as it should be, and be further away from the shortcomings of the program.

The differences between program theory and reality are not uncommon. This is another area that the evaluator needs to devote some attention. On one hand, without an understanding of the magnitude and nature of these differences, the evaluator may make some erroneous assumptions about the program theory. On the other hand, if the theory is so perfect that it does not depict reality, it needs to be revised. Suppose a drug treatment program calls for daily contacts between a drug counselor and participant. If the program resources do not allow for this, the program theory needs to be revised to account for meeting schedules that are realistic.

Because program theory is designed to capture reality, the corroboration of the program theory has to be confirmed by stakeholders and decision makers. Without their input the program theory may be irrelevant. Worse yet, the program theory may lead to an evaluation that cannot be useable. Another situation may arise. No corroboration of the definition of the program may lead to a poor definition of the program, or it could reveal competing philosophies between stakeholders and decision makers.

The evaluator needs a clear and concise description of the program theory. This is the guide to understanding the intentions of the program for proper analysis and evaluation. The corroboration of the program theory only serves as confirmation between stakeholders and decision makers that the program operates as intended. This does not place a good- or bad-quality statement on the program theory. For instance, Esbensen & Osgood (1999) argue that no part of GREAT explicitly discusses any criminological theory, but that different pieces of the GREAT curriculum capture parts of Gottfredson & Hirschi's (1990) self-control theory and Akers' (2009) version of social learning theory. Through corroboration and interviews with other academics and program staff this became clear. We will describe the steps for evaluating program theory next.

Analyzing Program Theory

Analyzing some type of program theory is common, and it usually takes place in a larger context of an evaluation of a program's process or impact. In the criminological and criminal justice literature, little has been written about how to perform an analysis. This is because it typically is performed in an informal manner that usually comes from commonsense judgments. When the program theory is articulated well, the validity of the program theory is straightforward and accepted on the basis of limited evidence or commonsense judgment.

Generally, programs are not based on simple expectations or goals. For instance, a parenting program that assigns case managers to coordinate courses for parents of children with low levels of self-control involves several assumptions about what it is supposed to accomplish and how (Piquero et al., 2010). In this situation, the program theory may be faulty, requiring a stringent evaluation or analysis.

Efficiency suggests that an analysis or evaluation of each individual assumption, goal, or objective of program theory may not be possible. This does not imply that these assumptions, goals, or objectives cannot or should not be subjected to evaluation or analysis. Certain tests exist that can be conducted to provide assurance that they are sound. Here, we summarize the types of tests that may be used to provide evaluation or analysis information.

Link between Program Theory and Social Needs

The program theory analysis and evaluation should begin with the needs evaluation as described in Chapter 3. This means that there needs to be a clear linkage between the program theory and the social need of the target participants. A program theory that does not have a link with social needs is an ineffective program no matter how well it is implemented; thus, one of the most fundamental issues is to analyze or evaluate the link between the program theory and social needs.

No set form of evaluation exists to determine if the program theory properly links to or generates a suitable conceptualization of how the social needs may be met. The proper evaluation process comes from the evaluator's judgment. To improve the validity of this type of evaluation multiple judgments from collaborators are necessary. The collaborators may be criminologists, policy makers, or advocacy groups associated with the target population.

The diversity of the group will make a contribution, but their chief contribution is specification. When program theory and social needs are described in general terms, the evaluator may have a false sense of congruence. For instance, when juvenile delinquency appears to rise during the summer months, some areas may institute a curfew barring juveniles from being out past a certain time. The social issue of juvenile delinquency appears to be solved by the program of a curfew. In reality, when the program theory or social need is vaguely written, the evaluator may have a false sense of service.

Greater detail is necessary to diagnose a social need and provide ample program theory for service. The diversity of the group may be able to bring experiences with other programs, knowledge from the criminological and criminal justice literatures, or knowledge of the political arenas for a better understanding. This will allow for a better program evaluation because the understanding of the social need is much better.

Moving forward to the program impact theory, it is instructive to remember that program impact theory is a sequence of causal links between program services and improved outcomes or benefits. The main issue is whether the program theory has had an impact or change on the social need that it is intended to alleviate from the needs evaluation. Consider for instance, a school-based educational program aimed at getting middle-school children to understand that gang involvement is a poor choice. The problem this program attempts to alleviate is gang membership. The program impact theory would show how linked educational modules raise the awareness of why joining a gang is a poor choice.

Evaluating Logic and Plausibility of Program Theory

Extracting and espousing the program theory should reveal the major assumptions and expectations of the program's design. One form of evaluation or analysis is a simple review of the logic or plausibility of the parts of the program. As with other forms of evaluation or analysis, a panel of reviewers should be brought together to help perform this type of evaluation or analysis of the program theory (Chen, 1990, 2011; Wholey, 1979, 1987). The panel should include members of the program staff, stakeholders, decision makers, and the evaluator. Because of the intimate relationship between these individuals and the program, it is advisable to involve informed individuals who do not have any connection to the program. This may include criminologists, other program administrators, or advocacy group members.

This type of evaluation is not a structured process—it should be open-ended. This does not mean that it should be without rigor. The rigor comes in some of the general issues that the review should address, including:

1. Are the program objectives well defined? The outcomes should be stated clearly and in a manner where a determination can be made as to whether the objectives have been met. A well-written objective is that a school offering an after-school program will reduce delinquency around the school during after-school

hours by 10%. The panel has a clear objective and a measurable outcome.
2. Are the program goals or objectives feasible? Is it possible that the program goals or objectives can be met? Completely eliminating crime is grandiose, but decreasing crime is much more attainable. The panel has the ability to determine if the goals or objectives are feasible.
3. Is the change process plausible? The program operates using a cause-and-effect format. That is, the program will cause a desired change for a proscribed group of participants. This implies that the program operates in a logical format resulting in a plausible change. The validity of the program theory is the ability of the causal logic of the program to produce intended effects. The most desirable situation would be that the causal logic within the program is supported by evidence that the logical links actually occur. The panel should be able to determine if the change process is plausible.
4. Are the procedures for identifying the target population, reaching them to deliver service, and sustaining the service through completion well defined or sufficient? Program theory should specify the procedures and functions that are sufficient for the purpose. This specification should come from two perspectives: the program's ability to perform and the target population's likelihood of being engaged. The panel should be able to identify these two things.
5. Are the resources allocated to the program and its various activities adequate? The resources for a program are vast. These resources include personnel, material equipment, and other assets (e.g., buildings, reputation, relationships, and facilities). The panel should be able to comprehensively identify the link between the program theory and resources.

Comparing Research with Practice

A method of assessing the program theory is to find out whether it is consistent with the research evidence or experience from elsewhere. The evaluator has numerous ways to be able to perform this type of comparison. The most straightforward manner is to evaluate a program using similar concepts. The results will provide information as to whether the program will be relatively successful. An evaluator should use evaluations of similar programs.

Other forms of research may be instructive as well. For instance, basic research in the criminological or criminal justice literatures may provide information about the program theory. The evaluator has to be very careful that a balance is struck between the basic research that does not have evaluation in mind and evaluation research.

Both will provide more information that will gain some insight into the program theory.

Summary

This chapter covers the basic information that is necessary for a criminal justice evaluator to complete a theory-driven evaluation. The assessment of evaluability is vital to the development of a theory-driven evaluation. To properly determine the evaluability of a program, the evaluator has to describe the program model, assess the opportunities for evaluating the model, and identify the stakeholders' interest in the model. This chapter also provides information about the production of program theory. The steps that are involved in the production of program theory result in a concise description of the program theory.

Discussion Questions

1. Identify a program from the criminal justice field. Work through the production of program theory. Discuss the issues that arise from completing the production of a program theory.
2. Discuss the steps in performing an evaluability assessment approach.
3. Discuss the differences among a program impact theory, service utilization plan, and program organizational plan.

References

Akers, R. (2009). *Social learning and social structure: A general theory of crime and deviance*. Boston: Northeastern University Press.
Chen, H. -T. (1990). *Theory-driven evaluations*. Newbury Park, CA: Sage.
Chen, H. -T. (2005). *Practical program evaluation*. Thousand Oaks, CA: Sage.
Chen, H. -T. (2011). *Practical program evaluation: Assessing and improving planning, implementation, and effectiveness*. Thousand Oaks, CA: Sage.
Chen, H. -T., & Rossi, P. H. (1980). The multi-goal, theory-driven approach to evaluation: A model linking basic and applied social science. *Social Forces, 59*, 106–122.
Chen, H. -T., & Rossi, P. H. (1983). Evaluating with sense: The theory-driven approach. *Evaluation Review, 7*, 283–302.
Coryn, C. L. S., Noakes, L. A., Westine, C. D., & Schroter, D. C. (2011). A systematic review of theory-driven evaluation from practice from 1990 to 2009. *American Journal of Evaluation, 32*, 199–226.
Esbensen, F. A., & Osgood, D. W. (1999). Gang Resistance Education and Training (GREAT): Results from the national evaluation. *Journal of Research in Crime and Delinquency, 36*, 194–225.
Gottfredson, M., & Hirschi, T. (1990). *A general theory of crime*. Palo Alto, CA: Stanford University Press.

MacKenzie, D. L., & Shaw, J. W. (1993). The impact of shock incarceration on technical violations and new criminal activities. *Justice Quarterly, 10*, 463–487.

Matthews, B., Hubbard, D. J., & Latessa, E. (2001). Making the next step: Using evaluability assessment to improve correctional programming. *The Prison Journal, 81*, 454–472.

Piquero, A. R., Jennings, W. G., & Farrington, D. P. (2010). On the malleability of self-control: Theoretical and policy implications regarding a general theory of crime. *Justice Quarterly, 27*, 803–883.

Rossi, P. H., Lipsey, M. W., & Freeman, H. E. (2004). *Evaluation: A systematic approach* (7th ed.). Thousand Oaks, CA: Sage.

Smith, M. F. (1989). *Evaluability assessment: A practical approach*. Norwell, MA: Kluwer Academic Publishers.

Van Voorhis, P., & Brown, K. (1996). *Evaluability assessment: A tool for program development in corrections*. Washington, DC: National Institute of Corrections. [Unpublished monography].

Van Voorhis, P., Cullen, F. T., & Applegate, D. (1995). Evaluating interventions with violent offenders. *Federal Probation, 50*, 17–27.

Welsh, W. (2006). The need for a comprehensive approach to program planning, development, and evaluation. *Criminology and Public Policy, 5*, 603–614.

Welsh, W., & Harris, K. (2004). *Criminal justice policy and planning* (2nd ed.). Cincinnati: LexisNexis: Anderson Publishing Co.

Wholey, J. S. (1979). *Evaluation: Promise and performance*. Washington, DC: Urban Institute.

Wholey, J. S. (1987). Evaluability assessment: Developing program theory. In L. Bickman (Ed.), *Using program theory in evaluation. New Directions for Program Evaluation, No. 33*. San Francisco: Jossey-Bass.

Additional Readings

Mercier, C., Piat, M., Peladeau, N., & Dagenais, C. (2000). An application of theory-driven evaluation to a drop-in youth center. *Evaluation Review, 24*, 73–91.

Wilson, D. M., Gottfredson, D. C., & Stickle, W. P. (2009). Gender differences in effects of teen courts on delinquency: A theory-guided evaluation. *Journal of Criminal Justice, 37*, 21–27.

5

PROCESS EVALUATION

Keywords
process evaluation
participant as observer
interviewing
focus groups

CHAPTER OUTLINE
Introduction 63
Process Evaluation: Program Implementation 64
Process Evaluation: Monitoring Conduct of Evaluation Research Design 66
Process Evaluation: Use of Qualitative Methods 69
  Evaluator: Participant as Observer 69
  Interviewing 71
  Focus Groups 73
Process Evaluation Assessment: Evidence-Based Correctional Program Checklist 75
Summary 76
Discussion Questions 77
References 77

Introduction

The first element of program evaluation is the process (implementation) evaluation. Here, three basic questions are pursued:
- Is the program providing its services as originally planned?
- Is the research design for the evaluation being carefully followed?
- Do any changes or alterations in either need to be performed?

The process evaluation is undertaken after the need for the program has been established and its theoretical foundation has been developed, tested, and refined (Mears, 2010, p. 133). It is concerned with initial program operations and whether the program is delivering its proposed services to its target population as originally planned—in other words, "what the program is and what it does" (Davidson, 2005, p. 56). Typically, the process evaluation is conducted to determine that the program was properly implemented before devoting time and effort to conducting the outcome evaluation. As Eck (2011, p. 11) notes, the process evaluation is all about accountability: Did the program come about as planned? Did all of its components work?

Process Evaluation: Program Implementation

The process evaluation focuses on both the monitoring of the program and the implementation of the original plan for it. Its purpose is to determine whether the program is being carried out as it was described in its original plan (typically in response to a grant application). Questions to be considered at this point include:

- Are the originally specified program operations applied as planned?
- Are the program resources adequate?
- Have staffing requirements for the program been met?
- Are the program goals being met consistently?
- Have any implementation problems and/or issues arisen?
- Has the program failed to reach and meet the needs of the target population?
- Is the program reaching the appropriate audience?
- How many individuals are receiving the services?
- What are the characteristics of the clients receiving the services?

During this process, the scope of the project and also of the evaluation research design should be reevaluated. As a result of this monitoring, some procedure or aspect of the program and/or evaluation research design may require corrective action and change. It makes obvious sense to redirect a program when it is going awry early in the process rather than assess the level of damage caused by its failure.

In a process evaluation, it is important to provide an accurate description of the program as it is implemented. The evaluator must directly observe the operations of the program upon implementation and talk directly with program administrators and staff. For example, returning to the adult drug court program example from Chapter 1, the evaluator should visit the court in operation and the location where treatment services are provided. When monitoring the implementation of police programs under the problem-oriented policing model, the evaluator should visit not only the police department but also the targeted area of the program to directly observe the nature of the crime problem. Limiting the sites of observation will also affect the quality, validity, and value of the information obtained via qualitative evaluation methods.

In addition, the evaluator should establish a schedule for conducting interviews and request all written reports and memos from the project itself. These data are valuable sources of information on program implementation. Thus, the process evaluation is a continuous and extensive undertaking that entails a detailed review of the entire period of program implementation. The aim is to provide a complete and comprehensive view of how the service provided by the program has been delivered. Here, the logic model (see Chapter 2) is especially helpful since the description of program operations should be compared to the program details listed in the logic model. It is the blueprint for program implementation, but if its implementation is not feasible or possible, changes to program operations are clearly in order.

A careful examination of the attributes of the program should be conducted. The evaluator conducts a diagnosis of program operations and its component parts to determine possible causes for the success or failure of the program itself (Suchman, 1987, p. 67). For example, one of the authors conducted an evaluation of an adult drug court program (Vito & Tewksbury, 1998). When he visited the treatment site for the program, he saw a sign that stated "A drug test will be given this Monday." Of course, such an announcement would tip off program clients who were abusing drugs to attempt to take steps to pass the test (e.g., bringing someone else's clean urine or dodging the test altogether). This obvious deficiency was pointed out to the program staff and it was quickly terminated. However, if the researcher had not visited the premises, it is likely that this problem could have become a normal component of the program's operations.

A second issue is whether the services are reaching the target population of clients whom the program was designed to serve. The main question is: Who is the program reaching and failing to serve, and why? Again, our experience with the adult drug court program evaluation provides an example. A review of the attributes of the clients who reached the drug court revealed that a large number of them were actually persons who dealt and sold illegal drugs but did not have a drug abuse problem. The program was initially designed for the diversion and treatment of drug abusers, not sellers who were "clean." Changes in screening clients were clearly in order. Drug sellers are illegal entrepreneurs, not addicts with a drug problem that leads them into crime. Thus, typical drug treatment programs do not address their problem. In fact, including drug dealers in treatment programs can give them the opportunity to reach more customers for their contraband goods.

Another vital purpose of the monitoring under process evaluation is to ensure that the program's implementation and proposed goals (especially its performance measures to determine effectiveness) are reasonable and realistic in light of changes in the program's environment. Specifications of the locale, timing, and auspices of the program should be made (Suchman, 1987, p. 67). In the adult drug court program example, changes in the nature of drug abuse among the clientele required changes in program operations. For example, if drug testing determines that cocaine is a major problem among clients, it may be necessary to limit the size of treatment groups for the purpose of more intensive counseling and observation of substance abuse levels through more drug testing in the program clientele. Program goals and measures of program effectiveness may require change in scope as a result of these adaptations in program operations.

Since it is impossible for the evaluator to foresee problems and issues that can arise during program implementation and the subsequent assessment of program effectiveness, the evaluator should develop a procedure to revisit and/or restructure project plans. The evaluator should specify when the reevaluation will occur. Of course, this feedback procedure must also be established with program administrators and operatives so they can be aware of and address problems that require attention.

Process Evaluation: Monitoring Conduct of Evaluation Research Design

At this point, the program evaluation should also monitor the implementation of the evaluation research design to determine whether it is being carried out according to the original specifications. Some key questions are:
- Are the required data being collected in a timely fashion according to the original research design?
- Are these data collected in an information system kept for the purposes of the evaluation?
- Has the original method of data analysis been maintained as proposed?
- Are management and evaluation reports being generated as planned?

To ensure the continued quality of the original evaluation research design, the evaluator should establish monitoring procedures in a regular and routine manner. Special attention must be given to the four questions just specified for quality control to be reliably established. Returning to the adult drug court program example, the evaluator may propose to visit the courtroom and treatment site every month to ensure that the program is underway as planned and that data and records are being properly collected and maintained. The evaluator may also wish to review all managerial reports about the program during its implementation. In addition, the information system for the program must be initially and immediately established. If data are not collected when clients enter the drug court, it may be very difficult to obtain information later in the evaluation process. In addition, these data are "perishable." It is better to obtain information about the nature and extent of a client's drug problem from both the program staff and the client as the client enters the program rather than to ask them to recall it at a later date.

Naturally, if the program is substantially changed, the evaluation research design will require alteration. The feasibility of the evaluation research procedures must be determined continuously. The originally established performance measures must be reassessed to ensure that they continue to be an adequate indicator of program performance. Thus, changes in the performance measures for the evaluation require the consideration of collecting new and additional data and determining the methods for collecting and processing them. As a result of the new data, modifications in the methods of analysis and a reexamination of the criteria for effective program performance may also be in order.

Some programs can change drastically upon implementation. For example, our experience evaluating a police-based rape prevention program revealed that it developed in unanticipated ways upon implementation. Originally, the performance measures for goals of the program were stated in this way:

- To increase by 10% the reporting of rape crimes that are cleared by arrest.
- To increase by 10% the proportion of rape arrests that result in conviction.

The program centered on the utilization of a specially trained counselor to deal with the problems associated with the crime of rape. Her office was formally tied to the police department. Typically, she was called to the scene of a rape (or other sex crime) to provide aid to the victim and to the police investigation of the crime. During the course of the program, she expanded her efforts to provide police training sessions on the emotional impact of rape on victims, as well as public education sessions to increase community awareness about the crime of rape. Thus, as it developed, the program changed to emphasize crime prevention rather than suppression, and the provision of services to victims (and potential victims) rather than arresting and convicting rapists. The evaluation research was transformed to collect information during an 18-month period about the number of times the rape counselor was called to the scene of a crime (103), occasions in which victim assistance was provided during the investigation (195), business calls received (1,081), calls received from victims (440), and contact hours spent with victims (1,051). Training sessions were held in all three police departments served by the program and 277 public information sessions were held for a total audience of 10,234. These measures documented the activity and productivity of the rape prevention specialist.

However, the formal goals listed here were still assessed, albeit in a different way—focusing on the cases in which the rape prevention specialist was included. Over the 18 months of the program, the rape prevention specialist was involved in 31 reported rape cases that resulted in 25 arrests (80.6%). Of these 25 arrests, 20 resulted in a conviction (80%) with 5 cases awaiting final outcome when the evaluation research was concluded. This conviction rate was substantially higher than that officially reported in the national crime statistics. According to those figures, the annual conviction rate for the county in question was only 18% (Vito, Longmire, & Kenney, 1983). Therefore, the activities listed here by the rape prevention specialist also had an impact on rape arrests and convictions. But the evaluation research revealed the existence of these ties through the process evaluation, not through an examination of the original goals of the program.

In sum, the process evaluation must formalize such methods of analysis. In particular, program management concerns should be addressed. These concerns include how implementation problems should be identified and corrected. The process evaluation should not only document the existence and nature of implementation problems but also the possible means of correcting them. This is necessarily a collaborative process among the evaluation researcher, program administrators, and operatives.

A second question is whether program modifications are in order, and how such alterations should be accomplished. If the goals of the program are not being met, potential operational changes must be identified and considered. Redirection of the program may still result in successful performance. Description, discussion, and analysis of the possible corrective actions should be part of process evaluation.

The final issue is whether these implementation problems are so serious that the program itself should be terminated. The recommendation to continue or terminate a program should be addressed in the process evaluation. At this point, if the research determines that the program will not achieve its performance goals at the end of the implementation period or fails to reach and serve its target population, program termination is a definite possibility. If it is impossible to make the necessary changes to redirect the program to a positive path, it should be terminated rather than continue a program that will ultimately prove ineffective. Thus, the process evaluation not only assesses implementation of the program, but can provide feedback information that can improve service delivery or halt it entirely.

Process Evaluation: Use of Qualitative Methods

Process evaluations must feature a detailed description of program operations and their implementation. This information can be obtained through direct observation and/or interviews with program administrators, staff, and clients (either directly or through the use of focus groups). Their perceptions will inform the process evaluation and provide information on program implementation (Patton, 1987, p. 23). After all, they are directly involved in the day-to-day operations of the program and have experience in considering its effective implementation. They have witnessed the program in action. The evaluation research must tap this invaluable source of information to fully assess the program.

Evaluator: Participant as Observer

Observation of program operations and implementation by the evaluator typically features the use of participant observation. In this case, the evaluator usually assumes the role of "observer as participant" where the research subjects (program administrators, staff, and clients) know the evaluator's role, identity, and purpose. The observations of the evaluator are overt and announced. Program administrators, staff, and clients know that the evaluator is present and that observations are being made. The evaluator is free to ask questions and directly observe program activities at any site and location. There is no need for the evaluation research to assume any other role or to hide the attempts at direct observation.

Methodologically, there are two basic drawbacks to this approach. First, the presence of the evaluator may alter the behavior of the persons under observation. To avoid this problem, the evaluator must become a routine and regular participant in program activities so that his or her presence is normal. A related problem is that the evaluator may develop strong ties to the groups studied and "go native"—that is, lose objectivity and become loyal to certain constituencies and elements of the program (Patton, 1987, p. 77). As Patton notes (1990, p. 209), "the ideal is to negotiate and adopt that degree of participation that will yield the most meaningful data about the program given the characteristics of the participants, the nature of staff–participant interactions, and the socio-political context of the program." If left uncorrected or addressed, these biases will damage the quality of the evaluation research design and its results.

In addition, Patton offers the following guidelines for process evaluation fieldwork (1990, pp. 273–274). First, he advises evaluation researchers to be descriptive in taking field notes and gather a variety of information from different perspectives. He also urges them to cross-validate and triangulate information by gathering different kinds of data (observations, interviews, program documentation, recordings, and photographs) by using multiple methods of qualitative research. It is wise to use quotations and thus represent program participants in their own terms. Evaluation researchers should capture participants' views of their experiences in their own words. Key informants must be selected wisely and used carefully and cautiously. Patton suggests drawing on the wisdom of their informed perspectives while keeping in mind that their views are limited and may be biased. Yet, key informants are people who are particularly knowledgeable and articulate, and their insights can prove particularly useful in helping an observer understand what is happening (Patton, 1987, p. 95).

Patton cautions evaluation researchers to be aware of and sensitive to the different stages of fieldwork. In the entry stage, it is important for them to build trust and rapport with all of the respondents—program administrators, operatives, and clients. Evaluation researchers need to remember that they are also being observed. Therefore, they must also stay alert and disciplined during the more routine, middle phase of fieldwork. They must guard against limiting or failing to make observations because they have become accustomed to the routine operations and events of the program under review. As the fieldwork draws to a close, they should focus on pulling together a useful synthesis of their observations. Overall, it is important for evaluation researchers to be disciplined and conscientious in taking detailed field notes at all stages of fieldwork and reviewing the notes promptly and carefully.

With qualitative methods, evaluation researchers must experience the program as fully as possible while maintaining an analytical perspective grounded in the purpose of the fieldwork. They are there to observe carefully while maintaining objectivity. A qualitative evaluation researcher must clearly separate description from interpretation and judgment. He or she should provide formative feedback for the program administrators that is carefully timed and verified. He or she should observe its impact that this feedback has on program operations. Yet, the researcher should also report his or ehr own experiences, thoughts, and feelings because those are also field data.

As the notes are compiled, certain categories of topics, issues, and relationships will become clear. The field notes will become structured around categories that inform the process evaluation. This information adds a distinct touch of reality to the evaluation research process, because it describes events in narrative fashion as they occurred and provides an invaluable supplement to any quantitative analysis of the program's efficiency and effectiveness in human terms.

Field observation was used by one of the authors in the process evaluation of a police department's anti-methamphetamine strategy. One aspect of the program was to conduct a public awareness campaign that featured the use of billboards to educate the public, increase their awareness about the dangers of methamphetamine, and make them aware of how they can report methamphetamine incidents to the police. The program contracted for anti-methamphetamine billboards, with five or more layouts to be displayed across the city. The evaluators visited all billboard locations utilized by the department. The majority of these displays were located close to the intersections of two roadways. However, the billboards were somewhat small and placed in areas where traffic was not truly substantial. As a result of this critical information, both the message and placement of the billboards improved dramatically during the second year of the project.

Interviewing

An interview is a structured conversation with an individual. The evaluator provides a format for the discussion by determining the questions to be asked, ordering them in a particular way, and determining the time and place of the interview. The aim is to ensure the accuracy of the information gathered during the interview. The assumption is that an interview will capture information that cannot be observed by the evaluator and tap into the subject's thoughts about the program, its operations, and its implementation.

According to Patton (1990, pp. 281-287), there are three basic approaches to interviewing. The first is the informal, conversational interview. This format features spontaneous questions, asked informally in the context of the process evaluation like anyone would in a typical conversation. Yet, the questions are predetermined by the evaluation researcher and vary according to the subject and setting. One of the advantages of this form of interview is that it gives the evaluator the greatest flexibility and responsiveness to differences in respondents and situations. Its informal nature is also less threatening to the respondent and thus makes the respondent more comfortable and able to engage readily in conversation. Among the disadvantages of this method is that the data collected from each subject may differ greatly. Therefore, the results may be more difficult to analyze. It also can take longer to collect systematic information when this method is utilized. Thus, an extended period of interviewing in the field setting is usually in order. Finally, this method may be easily affected by the conversational style of the interviewer. If the interviewer is very formal, he or she may be uncomfortable and ineffective using this style of questioning.

The second method of interviewing is the general interview guide approach. Here, the interview format is more formal than the conversational interview. The evaluator selects a series of issues to discuss with the research subjects prior to the interview. They have no specific ordering, but are used as a checklist of topics to be covered. There are several advantages to this method of interviewing. First, the information gathered through this method is similar for each respondent. This makes the results easier to analyze. While still systematic, the interviewing still gives the evaluator the flexibility to probe and explore responses when necessary. This type of interview is more efficient because the interviewer has some plan and thus uses time more efficiently. The disadvantages to this approach are similar to those of the informal interview. Although the process has more structure, the data are still conversational and informal and may be difficult to analyze. It is still easily influenced by the conversational and interviewing skills of the evaluator.

The third method is the standardized, open-ended interview. This style consists of a set of preestablished, carefully worded questions arranged in a specified order. The wording and ordering are developed with the intent of obtaining comparable responses from each subject. Thus, the foremost advantage of this method is that it minimizes variation in responses and makes the data more comparable and easier to analyze. This form of interview is the best and most efficient form to use when interviews are limited to one per subject and when the time for interviews is limited. There is also less potential for results to be influenced by the conversational style and technique of the interviewer. In terms of disadvantages to this approach, the interviewer's flexibility and ability to probe, explore, and expand on responses is limited. This problem may increase the chance that responses may be incomplete or misinterpreted. It also can reduce the interviewer's opportunity to take into account individual differences and variations in circumstances. The rapport between the interviewer and subject, as well as the quality of the responses, may be diminished as a result.

Overall, the fundamental principle of interviewing is that it should provide a structure in which the respondents can express their feelings and experiences in their own words. The method of interviewing should meet the needs of the respondent and the evaluator. If the respondents are not furnished with a comfortable interviewing framework, the quality and quantity of the responses will suffer. In process evaluations, the research subjects (program administrators, operatives, and clients) are viewed as informants—observers who possess specialized knowledge about the program and its operations, implementation, and effectiveness. The interview gives them the opportunity to state their opinions about program implementation and operations. Often they welcome this opportunity to "vent" in either a positive or negative way about how the program operates.

For example, another aspect of the public information campaign for the process evaluation of the anti-methamphetamine program noted before was through the use of public service announcements (PSAs) and ads on buses using mobile marketing. The combination of billboard displays, PSAs, and mobile marketing provided daily reminders of the dangers of methamphetamine use and manufacture to the community public. They also highlighted the methamphetamine tip-line phone number to report incidents of methamphetamine manufacture and abuse. The evaluators conducted interviews with the attendees at public methamphetamine abuse educational sessions. Participants disclosed they had heard and saw the radio and television PSAs. They also indicated that they had observed on numerous occasions the bus displays. Thus, the elements of the public information campaign appeared to reach the public and did not require alteration. Without this source of information, there was little or no opportunity to ascertain the impact of this marketing campaign.

Focus Groups

As discussed in Chapter 3, focus groups are a specialized method of interviewing where the researcher interviews a group of people at one time. A focus group is a group discussion usually consisting of 6–12 individuals. The discussion is used to obtain in-depth information from participants regarding attitudes, beliefs, behaviors, and opinions. The rationale for conducting focus groups is that opinions on day-to-day issues are not formed in a vacuum; rather, they are formulated and modified after discussions with others. The distinguishing advantage that focus groups have over the role of observer as participant or one-on-one interviews is the group dynamic that generates information that can be used as feedback from the process evaluation. A participant's articulation of his or her own view is aided by the opinions and beliefs of others. The group discussion process may help researchers achieve a richer understanding of the underlying issues and influences (Krueger & Casey, 2009, p. 8). Focus groups are typically conducted using an observer and a moderator. The moderator encourages discussion and the expression of differing opinions and points of view. The observer takes notes throughout the focus group session and generates a field report summarizing the discussion (Stewart & Shamdasani, 1998, p. 513).

One of the authors used focus groups in a study of the perceptions public housing residents held about a community policing program that was designed to combat drug dealing and violence (Walsh, Vito, Tewksbury & Wilson, 2000). The program aimed to identify ways that public housing authorities and local law enforcement officials could enhance the safety of citizens and combat rampant drug trafficking in the community's public housing complexes. A series of seven focus groups were conducted with residents of public housing complexes. In addition, surveys were administered door-to-door to a 10% sample of residents in the community being studied. While the surveys showed what percent of the residents reported that they had called the police in the last year, how frequently they saw police patrol in their community, how satisfied they were with police services, and whether they had personally participated in any of four crime prevention activities in the community, these data did not provide much information for the development of new programs, initiatives, or policies.

Here, the focus group interviews revealed residents had a strong sense of fear and attributed their fears, anxieties, and limitations on their out-of-home activities to a variety of active forms of intimidation practiced by the drug dealers operating in their neighborhoods. Focus groups also elicited a significant amount of data regarding residents' perceptions of and interactions with local law enforcement officials. While the survey data showed that 37% of residents had called the police for assistance in the previous year, the focus group data showed that residents were highly frustrated with the police response. Specifically, they felt that officers acted aloof, refused to stop when waved down by residents, would not leave their vehicles for conversations, treated residents with little or no apparent respect, and did not take their complaints seriously. As a result, residents did not envision the police as their allies for addressing local safety and crime problems. By engaging the residents of the public housing communities in conversations about their neighborhoods and whether or not the residents felt safe there, these patterns and themes emerged from the discussions. As a result, the researchers, public housing authority officials, and local law enforcement officials were provided with a fairly thorough understanding of why residents did not feel safe and why they failed to call the police when they witnessed a crime occurring. As a result, all three groups were able to identify and recommend changes for enhancing the safety (and overall quality of life) for these residents. Thus, this information from the process evaluation guided adjustments and changes in the program to improve service delivery and meet the original aims of the program. Data from the focus group revealed how the program was operating, including areas where improvements could be made and strengths of the program that should be maintained (Patton, 1990, p. 95).

Focus group interviews can also be used in other parts of the evaluation research. As discussed in Chapter 3, they can inform the needs assessment for the proposed program. It gives the target population of the proposed program the opportunity to state their grievances and problems in their own words and from their perspective. In the process evaluation, they can identify the strengths and weaknesses of implementation to inform necessary changes in service delivery. This information makes it possible to adjust program operations in a manner that can enhance program effectiveness. In the outcome evaluation, focus groups can give participants the opportunity to address the effectiveness of the program directly and once again provide information for the decision to alter, expand, or eliminate program operations (Patton, 1987, p. 136).

However, the focus group approach must be used with care. A group of offenders can really "feed" off of each other and one person can try to dominate weaker individuals. The research must take steps to prevent such domination and facilitate the participation of all persons in the focus group interview.

Process Evaluation Assessment: Evidence-Based Correctional Program Checklist

One method to conduct a process evaluation assessment is to use a scale to determine how well the program has been implemented. Developed by researchers at the University of Cincinnati in their analysis of over 400 programs, the evidence-based Correctional Program Checklist (CPC) is a tool to assess programs in terms of their capacity to deliver known principles of effective correctional intervention (Lowenkamp & Latessa, 2003).

The CPC is divided into two basic program areas: content and capacity. The capacity area is designed to measure whether a correctional program has the capability to deliver evidence-based interventions and services for offenders. There are three domains in the capacity area: leadership and development, staff, and quality assurance. The content area focuses on the substantive domains of offender assessment and treatment, and the extent to which the program meets the principles of risk, needs, client responsivity, and treatment. There are a total of 77 indicators, worth up to 83 total points that are scored during the assessment. Each area and all domains are scored and rated as either highly effective (65–100%), effective (55–64%), needs improvement (46–54%), or ineffective (<45%). The scores in all three domains are totaled and the same scale is used for the overall assessment score. It should be noted that not all of the three domains are given equal weight, and some items may be considered "not applicable," in which case they are not included in the scoring.

Data are collected through structured interviews with selected program staff and program participants, and observation of groups and services. In some instances, surveys may also be used to gather additional information. Other sources of information include a review of policy and procedure manuals, schedules, treatment materials, manuals, curriculums, a sample of case files, and other selected program materials. Once the information is gathered and reviewed the program is scored, and a report is generated that highlights the strengths, areas that need improvement, and recommendations for each of the three areas. Program scores are also compared to the average from across all programs that have been assessed.

The use of the CPC informs program operations in several ways. First, its indicators have been found to be correlated with reductions in recidivism. Second, the review process provides a measure of program integrity and quality, providing insight into the "black box" of a program. Third, it identifies both the strengths and weaknesses of a program and provides recommendations designed to improve the program's integrity and effectiveness. Thus, the CPC can provide valuable information to assess the capability of a program during a process evaluation.

Summary

There are three basic reasons why process evaluation is important. First, it can lead to improvements in both program design and implementation in a timely fashion. If the environment has changed or some unanticipated design flaws have been revealed as a result of the process evaluation, changes can be made to make the program relevant. Such changes are a result of the rational recognition that the program is not operating according to its original design, often through no fault of its own.

Second, process evaluations hold program administrators accountable because they provide a "summary judgment" of the initial performance and value of the program (Mears, 2010, p. 145). The process evaluation provides valuable feedback information on the initial program operations and performance by monitoring implementation. It can identify operational flaws and methods to correct them.

Third, process evaluations can inform the impact (outcome) evaluation by either validating or negating the performance measures and indicators established in the original program plan and evaluation research design. If they are in order, changes in performance indicators can be made to meet and address the issues revealed in the process evaluation. In sum, the monitoring functions performed by the process evaluation serve to regulate and ensure proper program operations and service delivery. A judgment must be made about the extent to which the program implementation followed and met its original plan. Analyzing how the program operates can thus inform the impact evaluation and explain program outcomes. A determination must be made as to whether implementation failure contributes to program failure (Harachi, Abbott, Catalano, Haggerty & Fleming, 1999). As noted, instruments like the Correctional Program Checklist can inform the process evaluation. A process evaluation combined with the impact evaluation of a program provides an opportunity to marry qualitative and quantitative methods to provide a more complete view of the program, its operation, and its clients (Sherman & Strang, 2004).

Discussion Questions

1. What are the purposes of a process evaluation?
2. Which areas and issues should a process evaluation include?
3. Why is program monitoring so important?
4. How does the evaluation research perform as a "participant as observer"?
5. What are the roles of interviews and focus groups in process evaluation?

References

Davidson, E. J. (2005). *Evaluation methodology basics: The nuts and bolts of sound evaluation.* Thousand Oaks, CA: Sage.

Eck, J. E. (2011). *Assessing responses to problems: An introductory guide for police problem-solvers.* Washington, DC: U.S. Department of Justice, Community-Oriented Policing Services.

Harachi, T. W., Abbott, R. D., Catalano, R. F., Haggerty, K. P., & Fleming, C. B. (1999). Opening the black box: Using process evaluation measures to assess implementation and theory building. *American Journal of Community Psychology, 27*(5), 711–731.

Krueger, R., & Casey, M. (2009). *Focus groups: A practical guide for applied research.* Thousand Oaks, CA: Sage.

Lowenkamp, C., & Latessa, E. (2003). *Evaluation of ohio's halfway houses and community-based correctional facilities.* Cincinnati: Center for Criminal Justice Research, University of Cincinnati.

Mears, D. P. (2010). *American criminal justice policy: An evaluation approach to increasing accountability and effectiveness.* New York: Cambridge University Press.

Patton, M. Q. (1987). *How to use qualitative methods in evaluation.* Newbury Park, CA: Sage.

Patton, M. Q. (1990). *Qualitative evaluation and research methods*. Newbury Park, CA: Sage.

Sherman, L. W., & Strang, H. (2004). Experimental enthnography: The marriage of qualitative and quantitative research. *The Annals of the American Academy of Political and Social Science, 595*, 204-222.

Stewart, D. W., & Shamdasani, P. N. (1998). Focus group research: Exploration and discovery. In L. Bickman & D. J. Rog (Eds.), *Handbook of applied research methods* (pp. 505-526). Thousand Oaks, CA: Sage.

Suchman, E. A. (1987). *Evaluative research: Principles and practice in public service and social action programs*. New York: Russell Sage Foundation.

Vito, G. F., Longmire, D., & Kenney, J. P. (1983). Preventing rape: An evaluation of a multi-faceted program. *Police Studies, 6*(4), 30-36. 50.

Vito, G. F., & Tewksbury, R. (1998). The Jefferson County (KY) drug court program: An impact assessment. *Federal Probation, LXII*(2), 46-51.

Walsh, W. F., Vito, G. F., Tewksbury, R., & Wilson, G. P. (2000). Fighting back in bright leaf: Community policing and drug trafficking in public housing. *American Journal of Criminal Justice, 25*(1), 77-92.

OUTCOME EVALUATION

Keywords

outcome evaluation
classic experimental design
experimental group
control group
statistical conclusion validity
internal validity
construct validity
external validity
descriptive validity
threats to internal validity
threats to external validity
quasi-experimental design
comparison group
self-drop group
propensity score matching (PSM)
before-and-after design
one-group time-series design

CHAPTER OUTLINE
Introduction 80
Classic Experimental Design 80
    Types of Validity 82
    Threats to Internal Validity 83
    Threats to External Validity 84
To Experiment or not to Experiment? 85
Quasi-Experimental Research Design 87
Before-and-After Design (One Group Pre-Test, Post-Test Design) 91
    One-Group Time-Series Design 92
Question of Causation 93
Summary 94
Discussion Questions 94
References 94

Policy makers live with a great deal of uncertainty. Unlike academics, they need to make decisions now, with the evidence available.
—John E. Eck (2006, p. 348)

Introduction

The purpose of the outcome evaluation is to determine whether a program, project, or policy has been effective and met its intended goals. The outcome evaluation must consist of a description of the analysis, how it will be implemented, and what the results mean. The design of the research is the most significant aspect. Comparisons must be made between the program participants (or area served by the program) and an "untreated" group. This key baseline gives meaning to the outcomes generated by the program by providing a comparison to what would have happened if the program had not been implemented.

Measures to determine the success of the project must be identified and developed to make this determination. Here, we are dealing with quantitative measures of success. Typically, they have two aspects. First, measures of program effectiveness are needed to help determine if the program was able to meet the needs of its target population. Second, efficiency measures (gleaned from the process evaluation) will gauge how well the program was implemented. Has it delivered the service(s) that it was designed to provide? Analysis of outcome evaluation data is critically related to the type of research design utilized by the program evaluator.

Classic Experimental Design

The classic experimental design features a crucial comparison in outcome results between the treatment (receives the services of the program) and the control (untreated) groups. The key feature is that the groups are selected *at random* from a pool of candidates from the target population that the program is designed to serve. Basically, the classic experimental design measures the impact of a program by applying it to the treatment group, withholding it from the control group, and then measuring what happened as a result of the experiment.

Here, random assignment is based on probability. First, the selection of cases must be independent. Every case must have an equal chance of selection and the selection of any one case cannot affect the probability that another case will be selected. It can be accomplished a number of ways from flipping a coin, to using a table of random numbers, to using the random number generation feature on a computer (Trochim & Donnelly, 2008, p. 239).

The purpose of random assignment is to guarantee that the two groups are equal and alike in every aspect except for their exposure to the program. That is the one and only difference between the groups that the classic experiment wishes to preserve and ultimately

Table 6.1 Classic Experimental Design

Group	Pre-test	Treatment	Post-test
Experimental group (R)[1]	T_1	X	T_2
Control group (R)	T_1		T_2

[1]Random assignment.

examine. The experimental group gets the program and the control group does not. Therefore, any difference in outcomes should be logically attributable to the exposure to the program and not due to other factors beyond the control of the evaluator. If there is a treatment effect, it should be present in the performance of the experimental group and not the control group.

Table 6.1 shows that after the subjects are assigned to the experimental and control groups, a pre-test (T_1) is given to both groups on the dependent variable, primarily to check for comparability. After exposure to the program (X, the treatment), the post-test (T_2) is given to both groups on the dependent variable. Then the difference in performance is determined and the appropriate statistical test is given to determine whether the difference is statistically significant (or greater than would be expected by chance). A comparison is made to determine whether this difference in performance favors the experimental group rather than the control group.

Boruch (1998) offers cautionary advice to program evaluators as they attempt to implement an experimental design. First, random assignment should occur as close as possible to the point of program entry. Second, it must be structured to meet the demands of the experiment and the field conditions of the program. The eligibility of the individual for the program must be determined prior to random assignment or there will be considerable time and effort wasted. Individuals may have to be grouped on the basis of demographic characteristics prior to random assignment (Boruch, 1998, p. 178). In short, the integrity of both the program and the classic experimental design must be maintained, which is not always an easy effort.

An evaluation of a drug court treatment program in Baltimore, MD, featured the use of an experimental design (Gottfredson, Najaka, Kearley, 2003). As reviewed in Chapter 1, the goal of a drug court treatment is to get offenders to abstain from drug abuse in the hope that they will then refrain from criminal behavior. In this study, drug offenders were randomly assigned to the drug court condition ($N = 139$, of which 67 performed in a certified drug treatment program for at least 10 days while the remaining 72 did not) and 96 were assigned to the control group. Review of background characteristics determined that these groups were similar with regard to race, gender, age, and prior criminal history. Therefore, the experimental and control groups were comparable and the random assignment to these groups was successful. Recidivism results determined that the "treated" drug court subjects had a lower rearrest rate over a two-year period (the operational definition of the dependent or outcome variable) (56.7%) than either the "untreated" drug court group (75%) or the control group members (81.3%) (Gottfredson, et al., 2003, p. 189). The use of an experimental design that ensured that these groups (including a second "untreated" group) were considered underscored the conclusion that the drug court was effective in reducing recidivism.

Types of Validity

Farrington (2003) contends that the methodological quality of a program evaluation is dependent on five criteria:

1. *Statistical conclusion validity:* This is concerned with whether the program intervention and program outcomes are related. The main threats to it are insufficient statistical power (the probability of rejecting the null hypothesis when it is false) and the use of statistical techniques that are inappropriate when the data violate the assumptions behind the statistical test (Farrington, 2003, p. 52).
2. *Internal validity:* This is whether the program intervention really did cause a change in program outcomes. Of course, the experimental design with the use of random assignment to experimental and control groups is the best mechanism to ensure internal validity.
3. *Construct validity:* This is the adequacy of the operational definition of program outcomes and other measurements in the program evaluation that track program interventions. Threats to construct validity include whether the program succeeded in making its intended changes in outcome (treatment fidelity or failure in program implementation); the validity and reliability of program outcome measures; ascertaining the level of crime displacement or the diffusion of program benefits; and contamination of the program treatment (control group exposure to the treatment) (Farrington, 2003, p. 54).
4. *External validity:* This is the generalizability of program findings to other settings. Of course, this is the purpose of systematic reviews of evaluations via the quality of their research design. The effect size of the program intervention is also a key indicator of value.

5. *Descriptive validity:* This is the adequacy of presentation of key evaluation features in the research report. Including previously mentioned indicators, evaluations should include such factors as the description of the treatment received, the follow-up period after the program intervention, and conflict-of-interest issues (e.g., Who funded the intervention? How independent were the researchers?) (Farrington, 2003, p. 55).

Primarily, the use of an experimental design helps the program evaluator to avoid problems with internal validity.

Threats to Internal Validity

Specifically, there are several types of internal (to the conduct of the experiment) validity problems (Cook & Campbell, 1979, pp. 51–55):

- *History:* This occurs when the research subjects experience an event in addition to the treatment that may affect their performance regarding the dependent variable.
- *Maturation:* The subjects may also change via biological or psychological processes rather than exposure to the program (treatment). For example, the experimental group may perform better or worse than the control group because they grew older, were fatigued, or were less interested in the program than they were when it began. Such changes would necessarily confound conclusions concerning the effectiveness of the program.
- *Testing:* Depending on the nature of the pre-test, it may be another treatment in itself. In the drug court example, this could be an issue if the pre-test was a drug test. Any difference in post-test drug testing results could thus be due to the initial drug test (and its outcome) and not due to the treatment portion of the drug court. In other words, if a person was positive on the first test, he or she would have an incentive to do better regardless of the effect of the treatment program.
- *Instrumentation:* Changing the instrument (or measurements) used between the pre-test and the post-test will also confound the issue of program effectiveness. Any outcome could be affected by these changes in addition to exposure to the treatment.
- *Statistical regression to the mean:* This is an issue when the target population represents an extreme group, like career criminals or repeat DWI offenders. Since the group is extreme in terms of its problem, they will get "better" just because it is unlikely that they can get any "worse." Therefore, some improvement in performance could be due to this source and program effectiveness.
- *Selection bias:* If any factors other than random assignment played a role in the assignment of individuals to the experimental

and control groups, selection bias is in play. For example, if individuals were referred to the drug court program because they were more amenable to treatment (i.e., were ready to change) rather than random assignment, the program could achieve good results due to this factor rather than any effort by program operatives. This is also known as *creaming*—selecting superior applicants to make the program look good (Boruch, 1998, p. 166).
- *Experimental mortality:* If individuals drop out of the experiment at high rates after it is underway, these losses could affect the results of the evaluation. For example, if drug court participants quit the program when they failed to pass a drug test, the experimental group may generate a lower recidivism rate on the post-test, not because of the drug court treatment but because the participants who did not abstain from drug abuse left the program, leaving those individuals who did succeed in the treatment group.
- *Masking:* The experimental treatment could have opposite or different effects on different kinds of subjects. For example, the drug court clients in the experimental group could have problems with different types of drugs (e.g., cocaine vs. marijuana or heroin vs. methamphetamine). Therefore, the drug court treatment may be more or less effective with its clients because of the source of their drug addiction (Adams, 1975, p. 69).
- *Contamination of data:* This occurs when the program evaluator loses control of the experiment and both the experimental and control groups are exposed to the treatment. For example, if the control group in the drug court experiment were somehow enlisted in some aspect of the program, the result would be that the evaluation now contained one larger experimental group and no control group (Adams, 1975, p. 70).
- *Erosion of the treatment effect:* This has to do with the gradual or abrupt disappearance of a successful performance of the experimental group in the early months after treatment (Adams, 1975, p. 70). For example, the treatment group in the drug court program could return to drug use following the program because they were no longer exposed to the treatment.
- Finally, outcome results could be affected by the *interaction of any of the preceding threats to internal validity*.

Taken as a whole, the program evaluator must address these problems as they occur with any type of research design. The classic experiment is not immune to these issues.

Threats to External Validity

In addition, the design of the research must also be concerned with its external validity—the generalizability or representativeness of the experimental findings. How can we be sure that the drug court program will register the same or similar successful results in another city or site as it did in Baltimore, MD?

To assess the external validity of a design, the program evaluator must also be concerned about (Cook & Campbell, 1979, pp. 73–74:

- *Interaction effects of selection bias:* In terms of the drug court example, clients of the program may have different types of drug problems, levels of addiction, and types of crime committed, not to mention differences in intelligence or socioeconomic status. Such differences could affect the confidence of the program evaluator that the drug court program will achieve the same results in another location.
- *Reactive effect of pre-testing:* A pre-test can increase the sensitivity of the research subjects. Again, if the drug court clients were given a drug test as a part of the pre-testing procedure for the drug court evaluation, they may be more or less aware of their potential to return to drug abuse. Therefore, the experimental group may no longer be comparable to those in need of the drug court program elsewhere.
- *Reactive effect of experimental procedures:* The experiment is a treatment in and of itself if the subjects become aware of the fact that they are being studied. Drug court clients may have altered their drug use because they were aware that they were part of the program evaluation. Therefore, they are no longer representative of the population that drug courts are attempting to reach.
- *Multiple treatment inference:* If the drug court treatment has several aspects (like drug counseling and drug testing), how do you know which of these treatment features were responsible for the results of the experiment?

The evaluator must be attentive to these threats to the generalizability of not only the research findings but also with respect to other settings, independent (treatment) variables, and outcome measures. The question is whether the findings of the outcome evaluation are applicable to other locations. In the public policy arena, this question is especially relevant. However, it must be stressed that all of the threats to validity (internal and external) can affect any type of research design utilized by a program evaluator.

To Experiment or not to Experiment?

There is a question of whether the quality of the research design of an evaluation report or study affects the nature of its findings. Weisburd, Lum & Petrosino (2001) reanalyzed data contained in the "Maryland Report" (see Chapter 1). They created a scale on studies from the report in terms of whether the investigator concluded that the program intervention had an effect (+1), no effect (0), or a backfire effect (−1). They then used the scientific methods scale from the "Maryland Report" to classify the research design for the study. Overall, they concluded that design does matter and that it has a systematic effect—the stronger the design, the more likely the study would report a positive treatment effect for the intervention, and the weaker the design, the more likely of a reported harmful treatment effect (Weisburd et al., 2001, p. 66). Thus, the strength of the research results is another argument in support of the use of the experimental design in program evaluation research.

Sherman (2007) advocates for the use of the experimental design on the basis that it will encourage the police to concentrate their scarce resources in the areas and on the offenders that produce the greatest amount of harm—the "power few." In addition, the results of an experimental design offer the most valid indication that the program itself is effective and not a source of harm itself. Focusing on the power few offers the greatest potential of generating a significant effect but also presents a paradox—"the best chance of a successful result may be found with the cases most likely to fail" (Sherman, 2007, p. 309). In a number of criminal justice examples, Sherman (2007) demonstrates that focusing on the power few does not ensure a treatment effect for the intervention (e.g., repeat-call address policing in Minneapolis). Nevertheless, the potential of this approach offers the best chance of success for a crime prevention intervention.

On the other hand, Eck (2006), who was one of the authors of the "Maryland Report," makes a case for the use and value of small-n evaluations in criminal justice program evaluation. He notes that researchers do not always have the time, resources, cooperation from policy makers, and expertise to mount an experimental design. Add to these issues the fact that the experimental design with random assignment requires considerable monitoring to be certain that the research protocol is followed. Also, the requirement of withholding treatment from the control group raises the possibility that a beneficial policy is being denied to some needy clients to maintain the integrity of the experiment, which is both an ethical and possible legal issue (Adams, 1975, p. 60).

Small-n evaluations have several advantages, especially that they can be implemented after the program has begun and are far less intrusive than experimental designs. The information that they can provide is valuable because they can help ascertain the effectiveness of crime prevention programs. Ultimately, rather than discard this information, the goals should be to include them in systematic reviews and hope that improvements in crime theory will also benefit small-n evaluations (Eck, 2006).

Indeed, not all of the research included in the "Maryland Report" exclusively featured an experimental design. Lum & Yang (2005) surveyed the authors of research articles and reports from the "Maryland Report" to attempt to determine why they chose to use experimental or nonexperimental methods to conduct their study. Overall, these researchers stated that while they believed that the experimental design with random assignment was the best approach to determine the effectiveness of a program or policy, practical reasons typically prevented them from adopting this approach. The ethical problems often raised by an experimental design (e.g., denial of treatment) did not emerge as a determining factor in using nonexperimental methods. The authors who did adopt an experimental approach noted that they had some previous experience with such designs and that the requirements of funding agencies often determined their use of an experimental design.

Palmer & Petrosino (2003) also offer several additional reasons for the abandonment of the experimental design in criminal justice evaluation research through their case study analysis of the California Youth Authority (CYA). The CYA established a strong research division that featured hiring Ph.D. researchers who obtained outside funding (notably from the National Institute of Mental Health) to conduct evaluations of the California Treatment Program through the use of experimental methods. However, both political and economic pressures conspired over time to move away from these methods. In particular, funding by the federal Law Enforcement Assistance Administration (LEAA) and the conservative emphasis on the "justice model" (that deemphasized rehabilitation as a correctional mission) led to the desire for policy-based results from quicker, short-term studies. Still, the CYA research division stands as a model example of a governmental agency that promoted experimental research and viewed objective information, data, statistics, and evaluation of programs as essential components in their decision-making process (Palmer & Petrosino, 2003, p. 256; see also Palmer, VanVoorhis, Taxman & MacKenzie, 2012). However, alternatives to the use of the classic experiment in evaluation research do exist.

Quasi-Experimental Research Design

The quasi-experimental design preserves the crucial comparison in program outcomes between a treated (experimental) and untreated group of program participants. It is typically applied when the setting does not permit the use of the classic experiment. Thus, the quasi-experiment attempts to maintain some measure of experimental rigor and control over relevant variables other than the treatment by some method except random assignment.

An article by Bonta, Wallace-Capreta & Rooney (2000) offers an example of a quasi-experimental research design used in the evaluation of an intensive rehabilitation supervision program in Canada. It featured three groups of offenders. The treatment (experimental) group received a cognitive behavioral program delivered in the context of intensive supervision in the community with electronic monitoring. In place of a control group, the quasi-experimental research featured the use of a comparison (untreated) group. This research featured two comparison groups. One comparison group consisted of untreated inmates who were selected from regions where electronic monitoring was unavailable. A second comparison group consisted of treated probationers who did not receive electronic monitoring. Both comparison groups were statistically matched with the treatment group with regard to risk and needs factors, plus they all met the selection criteria for electronic monitoring: conviction for a nonviolent and nonsexual offense, a sentence of less than six months, and an assessment of moderate risk (Bonta et al., 2000, p. 318). This matching process stood as a replacement for random assignment. However, in a quasi-experimental design, procedures like matching cannot Ensure comparability between groups with the same rigor as random assignment. With matching, the program evaluator can only be assured that the groups are comparable in terms of the variables used in the process—in this case, risk and needs factors. When random assignment is used, the program evaluator can be assured that the groups are alike in all possible aspects—those that can be measured and assessed and those that defy measurement and are unknown to the researcher.

Recidivism was operationally defined as a reconviction within one year of treatment completion or release from prison. A comparative analysis of the three groups determined that the intensive rehabilitation treatment group was less likely than the probationers to have committed a violent offense, but there were no differences between the three groups in their risk and needs assessment. The research findings determined that high-risk offenders who received relatively intensive levels of treatment had lower rates of recidivism (31.6%) than untreated high-risk offenders (51.1%) (Bonta et al., 2000, p. 325). Therefore, the research results revealed that the treatment was most effective with a particular type of program client—that is, high-risk offenders—a group that is traditionally difficult to treat and also could be subject to the internal validity threat of regression to the mean. However, electronic monitoring had little effect on recidivism for the experimental (treatment) group.

Thus, the quasi-experimental design attempts to ensure the similarity of the treatment and comparison groups and requires that only the experimental group is involved in the program. All of the previously mentioned threats to both internal and external validity apply to the quasi-experimental design and must be reviewed by the

Table 6.2 Quasi-Experimental Design

Group	Pre-test	Treatment	Post-test
Experimental group	T_1	X	T_2
Comparison group	T_1		T_2

program evaluator. The elements of the quasi-experimental design are presented in Table 6.2. Again, the only difference between the classic and quasi-experimental designs is the manner in which the untreated comparison group is constructed. In fact, the term *comparison group* clearly indicates that random assignment was not used to construct it; the term *control group* is reserved for the classic experiment where random assignment is used to determine group participation.

There are several possible ways to construct a comparison group. In the preceding example, two comparison groups were used:

1. A geographically ineligible inmate group (electronic monitoring was not available in their area).
2. An untreated probation group.

Both groups were then statistically matched in terms of risk and needs factors to ensure that they were comparable in those regards.

Another method suggested by Adams (1975, p. 62) is the use of a self-drop group. He describes the evaluation of a prison college quasi-experiment were the comparison group consisted of inmates who had applied for the college program but had been released from prison or otherwise diverted before they were admitted to the program. It is significant that these inmates were not officially denied access to the program because that would be a source of selection bias. They did not participate for nonprejudicial reasons of their own: they had been paroled earlier than expected, entered other programs while waiting and did not want to drop them, or changed their minds while waiting.

Self-drop groups have been featured in several correctional program evaluations. A jail-based education program evaluation featured the use of a self-drop group of inmates who were eligible for the program but did not choose to participate because they were involved with other programs like work release. The research results revealed that program participants significantly increased their reading and math levels in comparison to the scores of the self-drop group (Tewksbury & Vito, 1994, pp. 57–58). A self-drop group was also used in an evaluation of a drug court program. Here, it consisted of convicted persons who had been screened for the program but elected not to enter it. The evaluation research results determined that drug court graduates had the lowest rate of reconviction (13.2%) compared to both drug court nongraduates (59.5%) and members of the self-drop group (55.4%) (Vito & Tewksbury, 1998, p. 50). However, in both of these examples a common threat to validity existed. Program participants in both the jail and drug court programs volunteered to participate. Therefore, their motivation to succeed may have been higher than that of the members of the self-drop groups.

Another method of constructing an equivalent comparison group in a quasi-experimental design is through the use of propensity score matching (PSM). PSM is designed to reduce the selection bias that is often a problem in quasi-experimental design. The propensity score is generated via a logistic regression model that estimates the probability of group selection. Selection into the treatment group (0 = no selection; 1 = selection) is the dependent variable in the logistic regression model. Thus, PSM creates treatment and comparison groups by using the likelihood of observed characteristic in the groups (i.e., independent variables like race, gender, age, drug history, criminal offense, etc.) and balances the groups in terms of these observed characteristics (Duwe, 2010, p. 50; Higgins, Ricketts, Griffith, Jirard, 2013, p. 5).

Duwe (2010) conducted an evaluation of a prison-based drug treatment program in Minnesota that featured a quasi-experimental design with the use of PSM to construct treatment and comparison groups ($N = 926$ in each group). The average follow-up period was 48 months and recidivism was calculated as rearrest, reconviction, or reincarceration during this timeframe. The analysis revealed that involvement in the prison drug treatment program reduced the risk of recidivism by 17–25% and completing it reduced recidivism by 20–27% (Duwe, 2010, p. 79).

Use of PSM was also featured in a drug court evaluation in Vancouver, Canada (Somers, Currie, Moniruzzaman & Patterson, 2012). Participants were enrolled in the drug court program between 2001 and 2008 and the follow-up period for measurement of recidivism was 24 months. The independent variables used by PSM to establish the treatment and comparison groups ($N = 180$ for both groups) were both traditional (age, gender, ethnicity, education, risk/needs assessment variables, correctional history) and innovative (involvement in community health services for either a drug or mental health disorder, number of hospital days in the two years prior to drug court, involvement in drug or alcohol community treatment services, and social assistance provided in the two years prior to drug court involvement). Recidivism analysis provided evidence of drug court effectiveness. Drug court clients had a reduction of 0.95 in offenses per year and also for drug-related offenses (0.42 per year). The number of drug court participants who were sentenced for drug-related charges decreased by over 50% in the two years following drug court enrollment (Somers et al., 2012, p. 398).

These examples reveal that PSM offers a unique and robust method of constructing treatment and experimental groups in a quasi-experimental design where random assignment is not feasible. In a quasi-experimental design, PSM allows us to estimate the probability of a person's inclusion in the treatment or comparison group through the use of a statistical model of the variables that account for the propensity of a study participant to be in one of the groups. The propensity score is defined as the probability (from 0 to 1) of group membership based on a set of covariates that predict membership in one of the groups. The success of this strategy is most likely if the set of relevant predictor variables (e.g., the independent variables used in the studies mentioned before) has been thoughtfully considered (Trochim & Donnelly, 2008, p. 329).

Before-and-After Design (One Group Pre-Test, Post-Test Design)

Criminal justice policies and programs are often analyzed after they are implemented. Thus, researchers have no control over the time and places where the policies are instituted. Despite this issue, the impact of criminal justice policies can be reviewed to determine whether they were effective in terms of the intent of the policy.

This design features the comparison between the performance of the same group before (pre-test) and after (post-test) exposure to the experimental treatment (X), as shown in Table 6.3. However, it is a weak type of design because the researcher will be unable to be certain that the experimental treatment (X) is responsible for the difference (if one exists) before and after the measurement is taken. The only comparison made is within the experimental group. Thus, the effect of the treatment is determined by comparing what happened before and after the treatment was implemented (Reichardt & Mark, 1998, p. 200). In sum, it represents the first half of a quasi-experimental design.

Here, let us examine the impact of a policy designed to increase the deterrent effect of the Kentucky Youthful Offender Act. The intent of this act was to get tough on juveniles who committed homicide so that these offenses would decrease. Vito & Keil (2004) used a pre-test/post-test design to determine whether juvenile homicidal behavior changed (in terms of deliberation, randomness, and viciousness)

Table 6.3 Before-and-After Design

Group	Pre-test	Treatment	Post-test
Experimental group	T_1	X	T_2

Table 6.4 One-Group Time-Series Design

Group	Pre-test	Treatment	Post-test
Experimental group	T_1, T_2, T_3, T_4	X	T_5, T_6, T_7, T_8

following the passage of this act. Therefore, the introduction of the law constituted the treatment (X) variable. Specifically, the act lowered the age requirement for youths to be transferred to adult court where they could be eligible for capital punishment. The analysis determined that the act had little impact on juvenile homicidal behavior and that juries were no more likely to impose the death penalty on juvenile offenders.

One-Group Time-Series Design

An expansion of the before-and-after design is the one-group time-series design, which features more frequent measures taken before and after the introduction of the treatment (X) variable (Table 6.4). The use of several tests given over a time period gives the researcher more control over possible threats to internal validity than the before-and-after design.

Using this type of design, another study analyzed the impact of the U.S. Supreme Court decision that outlawed the execution of juveniles (*Roper v. Simmons*) on the number of homicides committed by juveniles in 20 states (Flexon, Stolzenberg, D'Alessio, 2009). Thus, this study expanded on the research question proposed by the Vito & Keil study (2004): Did a change in juvenile homicide policy affect the number of these offenses committed? First, the analysis was much broader in its scope. It used nationwide data on homicides from the "Supplemental Homicide Report" maintained by the Federal Bureau of Investigation under its Uniform Crime Reporting Program. Second, because the Vito & Keil study (2004) was a before-and-after design, it only examined one point in time, so it was less sensitive to variations in the juvenile homicide rate than a time-series design would be. The time-series analysis conducted by Flexon & colleagues (2009) extended the study of this topic through the use of this more sophisticated design.

They utilized an ARIMA (auto-regressive integrated moving average) model to consider several points in time before and after the *Roper v. Simmons* decision. This type of model is collected over time both before and after the treatment is implemented (in this case, the court decision). The trend in the pre-treatment measurements is projected forward in time and compared with the post-treatment measurements. It is most effective when the effect of the treatment is likely to be relatively immediate and abrupt (Reichardt & Mark, 1998, p. 210). The research determined that the repeal of the juvenile death penalty had no observable impact on homicides committed by juveniles (Flexon et al., 2009, p. 942). Therefore, both studies concluded that expanding the scope of capital punishment for juveniles or removing it entirely made no difference in the rate of homicides committed by juveniles.

Question of Causation

After considering and adopting the research design and conducting the analysis, one key question remains: How confident is the evaluator that the program was responsible for the final outcome obtained?

Eck (2011, pp. 19–23) offers four criteria for assessing cause:

1. *There is a plausible explanation of how the response reduces the problem.* Here, the theory behind the program treatment and the review of previous research on the subject will help the evaluator make a determination. He or she still needs to show how the program succeeded, under what conditions, and whether the program response was generally useful.
2. *The response and the level of the problem are related.* Basically, is there a relationship between the program response and a favorable outcome in the impact evaluation results? As Eck (2011, p. 20) states to claim causation here, an evaluator must "demonstrate that the problem is bigger in the absence of the response than when the response is in place."
3. *The response occurs before the problem declines.* This is the requirement of causal time order—namely, that the program response must precede the decline in the problem (see also Cook & Campbell, 1979, pp. 53–54). Thus, it is necessary to measure the extent of the problem prior to and following the implementation of the program—the basic elements of the before-and-after design.

4. *There are no plausible alternative explanations.* In other words, the evaluator must eliminate "rival" causal hypotheses and determine whether anything else was responsible for the program outcomes.

Consideration of these issues will help strengthen the impact evaluation results and conclusions.

Summary

Outcome evaluations help us determine the effectiveness of a program or policy. To do so, they must be carefully constructed to ensure that valid comparisons are made between the program (or policy) and what would happen if it were not implemented. The crucial task for the program evaluator is to construct and maintain the integrity of the best possible research design available to make this assessment. The impact of a policy or program is difficult to ascertain when these issues are not carefully attended to.

Program evaluators should attempt to rule out threats to validity by adding comparisons that put the validity and impact of the treatment into direct competition. In other words, the program evaluator must plan ahead and anticipate the need for additional comparisons to evaluate the threats to validity (Reichardt & Mark, 1998, p. 224). The construction of a valid research design is the most important function of the program evaluator. It is here that the program evaluator contributes to the decision-making process by ensuring that valid data are provided and relevant comparisons are made to determine if the program has been effective or how it has failed.

Discussion Questions

1. What is the purpose of outcome evaluation?
2. What are the elements of the classic experimental and quasi-experimental designs? How are they similar? How do they differ?
3. What are the threats to internal validity?
4. What are the threats to external validity?
5. What is propensity score matching and what are its benefits?

References

Adams, SA. (1975). *Evaluative research in corrections: A practical guide.* Washington, DC: U.S. Department of Justice.

Bonta, J., Wallace-Capreta, S., & Rooney, J. (2000). A quasi-experimental evaluation of an intensive rehabilitation supervision program. *Criminal Justice and Behavior, 27*(3), 312–329.

Boruch, R. F. (1998). Randomized controlled experiments for evaluation and planning. In L. Bickman & D. J. Rog (Eds.), *Handbook of applied social research methods* (pp. 161–192). Thousand Oaks, CA: Sage.

Cook, T. D., & Campbell, D. T. (1979). *Quasi-experimentation: Design and analysis issues for field settings*. Boston: Houghton Mifflin.

Duwe, G. (2010). Prison-based chemical dependency treatment in Minnesota: An outcome evaluation. *Journal of Experimental Criminology, 6*, 57–81.

Eck, J. E. (2006). When is a bologna sandwich better than sex? a defense of small-*n* case study evaluations. *Journal of Experimental Criminology, 2*, 345–362.

Eck, J. E. (2011). *Assessing responses to problems: An introductory guide for police problem-solvers*. Washington, DC: U.S. Department of Justice Office of Community-Oriented Policing Services.

Farrington, D. P. (2003). Methodological quality standards for evaluation research. *Annals of the American Academy of Political and Social Science, 587*, 49–68.

Flexon, J. L., Stolzenberg, L., & D'Alessio, S. J. (2009). Cheating the hangman: The effect of *Roper v. Simmons* decision on homicides committed by juveniles. *Crime and Delinquency, 57*(6), 929–949.

Gottfredson, D. C., Najaka, S. S., & Kearley, B. (2003). Effectiveness of drug treatment courts: Evidence from a randomized trial. *Criminology and Public Policy, 2*(2), 171–196.

Higgins, G. E., Ricketts, M. L., Griffith, J. D., & Jirard, S. A. (2013). Race and Juvenile incarceration: A propensity score matching evaluation. *American Journal of Criminal Justice, 38*(1), 1–12.

Lum, C., & Yang, S. M. (2005). Why do evaluation researchers in crime and justice choose non-experimental methods? *Journal of Experimental Criminology, 1*, 191–213.

Palmer, T., & Petrosino, A. (2003). The "Experimenting Agency": The California youth authority research division. *Evaluation Review, 27*(3), 228–266.

Palmer, T., VanVoorhis, P., Taxman, F. S., & MacKenzie, D. L. (2012). Insights from ted palmer: Experimental criminology in a different era. *Journal of Experimental Criminology, 8*(2), 103–115.

Reichardt, C. S., & Mark, M. M. (1998). Quasi-experimentation. In L. Bickman & D. J. Rog (Eds.), *Handbook of applied social research methods* (pp. 193–228). Thousand Oaks, CA: Sage.

Sherman, L. W. (2007). The power few: Experimental criminology and the reduction of harm. *Journal of Experimental Criminology, 3*, 299–321.

Somers, J. M., Currie, L., Moniruzzaman, A., & Patterson, M. (2012). Drug treatment court of vancouver: An empirical evaluation of recidivism. *International Journal of Drug Policy, 23*, 393–400.

Tewksbury, R. A., & Vito, G. F. (1994). Improving the education skills of jail inmates: Preliminary program findings. *Federal Probation, LVIII*(2), 55–59.

Trochim, W. M., & Donnelly, J. P. (2008). *Research methods knowledge base*. Mason, OH: Atomic Dog.

Vito, G. F., & Keil, T. J. (2004). Dangerousness and the death penalty: An examination of juvenile homicides in Kentucky. *The Prison Journal, 84*, 436–451.

Vito, G. F., & Tewksbury, R. A. (1998). The impact of treatment: The Jefferson County (Kentucky) drug court program. *Federal Probation, LXII*(2), 46–51.

Weisburd, D., Lum, C. M., & Petrosino, A. (2001). Does research design affect study outcomes in criminal justice? *Annals of the American Academy of Political and Social Science, 578*, 50–70.

COST-EFFICIENCY EVALUATION

Keywords
cost-benefit analysis
cost-effective analysis
rate of return
opportunity cost

CHAPTER OUTLINE
Introduction   97
Costs   99
   Types of Costs   100
      Direct versus Indirect   100
      Recurring versus Nonrecurring   100
      Hidden versus Obvious   101
      Opportunity   101
      Variable versus Fixed   101
      Incremental versus Sunk   102
   Why Examine Costs?   102
   Outcomes to Costs   103
   The Heart of Cost-benefit Analysis   103
   The Heart of Cost-effectiveness Analysis   104
   Issues of Cost Analyses   105
   Unit of Analysis   105
   What Do Future Costs and Benefits Hold?   106
   Paying Costs and Reaping Benefits   107
   Using Cost-benefit and Cost-effectiveness Analysis   107
Limits of Cost Analyses   108
   Value of Life   108
   Assumptions and Cost Analysis   109
Summary   109
Discussion Questions   109
References   110

Introduction

Program evaluations have to consider cost. An evaluator may have devised the best needs assessment, process evaluation, and impact or outcome evaluation that can positively impact the lives of those the program is intended to impact, but the program may have a negative impact if the costs exceed what society is willing to pay or exceed the cost of alternative programs that can resolve the same problem. Without this information, proposed programs are nothing more than recommendations or philosophy without a statement of the costs; thus, the program should not be taken seriously. Evaluators should link program outcomes to costs if the results of the evaluation are to be useful in making decisions. As the criminal justice environment (i.e., crime, court proceedings, imprisonment, and treatment) becomes more expensive, efficiency is an important issue, and costs are relevant to gauge necessary changes. Individuals working in the criminal justice environment do not usually have the capacity, training, or understanding of cost-effective evaluation, leaving them in a naive state of the effectiveness of programming. The issue becomes even worse when considering professors, who often serve as external evaluators. Most do not have a full understanding of cost effectiveness and its relationship to outcomes.

Cost analysis is not new to criminal justice evaluations. Most of the methodologies that evaluators use come from the business and economic fields (Thompson, 1980). An example of a business taking into account cost-effective analysis is a store owner who counts the dollar value of sales receipts and compares the value to costs (e.g., salaries, utilities, inventory, shipping, infrastructure, etc.). This process provides the store owner some indication of whether the store is making or losing money. While this example seems very simple, in the criminal justice environment, this process is not as simple. The criminal justice environment does not usually sell anything, but, mostly, gives away its products (i.e., arrest, trial, or prison) or programming (i.e., treatment, education, or training). The tax payer usually pays the expenses, and the individuals working in the criminal justice environment have a difficult time converting the benefits of their products or programming into dollars.

Costs analyses are important at two parts of the program process. In the planning stage, projecting the costs of a potential program and matching them to its intended objective(s) is important before implementation (Royse & Thyer, 1996). An understanding of the costs will help determine if the program is feasible. For instance, the former "weed-and-seed" programs operated using three pieces. One piece is overtime for law enforcement so that they may "weed" the area of the criminal element. Another piece is the community developing programs to "seed" a prosocial element in a community. The final piece is a voluntary advisory board to orchestrate the weed-and-seed efforts. The law enforcement piece (weed) and the community programming piece (seed) have to operate using a specified budget, and the advisory board is the manager of the budget. To properly operate a weed-and-seed program, the advisory board has to have a firm grasp of the overtime costs and the community programming costs. In some instances, many weed-and-seed programs were not able to sustain or properly implement many potentially wonderful programs because they did not understand the cost parts of programming.

To avoid these types of issues, the evaluator before implementation may address several questions to assist in understanding the feasibility of a program, including:
- What are the personnel costs?
- What are the costs for infrastructure (e.g., cars, computers, or buildings)?
- Are there transportation costs for the client?
- Are there utility (e.g., phones, electricity, or water) costs for the infrastructure?
- Will overtime be necessary?
- What are the costs to the criminal justice system?

Few will implement a program without some type of justification for spending the funds. After the program implementation, evaluators must assess the quality of the program's implementation and impact (as discussed in earlier chapters) in the context of the program costs. After the program implementation has occurred, cost effectiveness is important because it allows the public, organization, and program participants (i.e., employees, administrators, and sometimes clients) to understand the success or failure of the program in the context of the costs of the program. For instance, a program may work wonderfully and provide a substantial impact for the individuals who it is designed to help. The program, however, may cost so much that it is not possible to continue to operate it. The optimal situation is to have a strong impact, and be affordable to society to continue to operate. Unless the cost-effective analysis is performed after the program has been implemented, this will not be known.

To delve into the performance of a cost-effectiveness evaluation the remainder of this chapter will discuss methodologies that evaluators commonly use to examine the cost effectiveness of programs at these two stages.

Costs

Because of the lack of training and education in this area, evaluators need some mechanism that they can use to organize their efforts in determining the costs of a program. One effective organization method is to use categories. Categories make clear the necessary pieces for understanding the types of costs for an analysis.

Table 7.1 Cost Categories

Direct versus indirect
Recurring versus nonrecurring
Hidden versus obvious
Opportunity
Variable versus fixed
Incremental versus sunk

Types of Costs

In planning a program, evaluators take into account six different categories of competing costs shown in Table 7.1. It is instructive to keep in mind that all of these are not mutually exclusive. For instance, salaries are a direct cost, but they are a recurring cost. This means that an evaluator has to make a decision for how to place items in the categories. This suggests that the categories are subject to debate. The settlement for the debate depends on the purpose of the program evaluation. For example, if an evaluator is examining the direct costs for a correctional program, salaries may be included as a direct cost. However, the evaluator has to understand that this is also a recurring cost, but it may be categorized this way because the focus of the evaluation is for direct costs.

Direct versus Indirect

Direct versus indirect costs are an important issue to consider in the planning of a program. Specifically, the planner needs to consider the costs that associate with providing services and the support costs that make providing the services possible. To provide services, or direct cost, consider the salaries of the service provider and all other management issues (e.g., receptionist, telephones, computers, Internet access, lease of office or building space, etc.). Planners have to take the direct costs into account to make sure that the program is able to continue providing the service. Indirect costs are the issues of overhead. Planners have to consider both of these costs to properly implement the program.

Recurring versus Nonrecurring

Recurring versus nonrecurring costs is another important issue to resolve in the planning stages of a program. Recurring costs come about on a regular interval. Examples of these types of costs are salaries, rent, taxes, and utilities. Nonrecurring costs are for items that do not require interval-style purchase. In other words, the purchase of a computer should last a number of years; thus, it is a nonrecurring cost because it does not require interval purchasing.

Hidden versus Obvious

Hidden versus obvious costs are important to consider when a program is being planned. The issue here is to slow down planners in their consideration of costs. Planners need to move slowly because the distinction between hidden and obvious costs is nothing more than costs that are easily recognizable. Hidden costs require a great deal of inquiry and research. A planner may have to perform some type of qualitative interviewing or survey research to make sure that a cost was not overlooked. For instance, when expanding a program's staff, the planner has to keep in mind that this entails more than just salaries—it also means that fringe benefits and insurance costs have to be considered as well. These may seem obvious, but in the middle of busy times, these costs can be overlooked.

Opportunity

Opportunity costs are critical to the planning and implementation of a program. Planners have to consider the cost of the program being considered and the cost of other programs. This will allow the planner to better understand the choices between the considered program and alternative programs. For instance, a community that has a drug issue with teenagers may wish to implement some type of drug education for reduction purposes. The adoption of D.A.R.E. without considering other programs (e.g., traditional health curriculum) means that the opportunity for a more cost-effective program adoption may have been lost. In other words, the adoption of D.A.R.E. may make it impossible for a criminal justice organization to serve other important needs of a community.

Variable versus Fixed

Variable versus fixed costs is also important consider. These costs represent the amount of money necessary to simply open the doors of the organization. When considering these types of costs, think of predatory mortgage lending and mortgage interest rates. During the mortgage crisis in 2008, many individuals were given mortgages that they could not afford. The problem affording these mortgages occurred because variable mortgage interest rates, known as adjustable-rate mortgage (ARM), fluctuated when other interest rates changed. For instance, someone using an ARM may pay 3% one month and 14% the next month; the individual could easily afford 3% but the 14% becomes unrealistic. As a side note, this type of mortgage lending is known as predatory lending and is now illegal. Others may have a fixed-rate mortgage. This means that the individual began their mortgage at 3% and it remains 3% for the life of the mortgage.

Incremental versus Sunk

Incremental versus sunk costs are important to planners because they can have different influences on the yearly, monthly, and daily budgets of a criminal justice organization. With this in mind, future behavior or decisions should rely on incremental costs rather than sunk costs. Incremental costs reflect the amount of funds that the organization expends on a daily basis—salaries or repairs. Sunk costs are those that have been previously expended. For instance, when a correctional facility purchases a vehicle to transport an inmate, the original cost of the vehicle compared to the current value of the vehicle is the sunk cost. The daily expenditure is the most proximal cost feature for a decision maker or evaluator. While sunk costs are important they are usually one-time costs, but incremental costs occur more than once.

Why Examine Costs?

Criminal justice organizations cannot ignore the costs of programs. The scarce amount of funds means that evaluators are always making choices. For instance, a county instituted a drug treatment program to improve the quality of lives of drug addicts, and to provide services that may postpone jail sentences. The evaluators discovered that even though the treatment program is a good idea, only a small percentage of those eligible attended the program. Depending on the assumptions of cost, the operational cost of the drug treatment program is more than educating a school child. Therefore, the drug treatment program costs more than the value of the services.

The drug treatment program cost analysis is part of an operational evaluation of the program. Planners will also try to project costs of programs during the planning stage. Planners may have difficulty projecting these costs creating errors. Sometimes a program does not attract as many participants as anticipated, or the program may attract more participants than anticipated. A community decides to build a jail. The contract bids suggest that the jail will cost in the low millions to build. After building the jail, however, the final cost was 1 billion dollars. Not having an accurate projection of the cost of the jail may take away funds for other projects or programs. Not meeting other needs is an opportunity cost.

Outcomes to Costs

The determination of the costs is only part of the process. As it turns out, it is the easiest part of the process. Thinking about the preceding types of costs, each will come with some type of tangible notation (i.e., bill) for payment daily, weekly, monthly, or yearly. Even with adequate research exposing potential hidden cost issues, the actual cost of every piece of a program is relatively easy to estimate or have precise information.

The difficult part of the process is the determination (i.e., estimate or have precise information) of benefits. Benefits are difficult to determine since they are complex because of multiple ways to determine them, and their goals are usually not easily or clearly presented. Benefits are the result of a program achieving its goals. For example, vehicle take-home programs improve the productivity of law enforcement officers keeping the community safe (Lauria, 2007).

When determining benefits it may be easier to think about the amount of money available if the money has not been spent. For instance, take into consideration all of the money that a correctional institution may have if it did not offer drug treatment programming. An evaluator can contrast the average time to relapse upon release from a correctional institution with those who completed a drug treatment program. Common knowledge suggests those who did not have access to a drug treatment program are likely to relapse sooner than those who did have access. Those who relapse are likely to come into contact with the criminal justice system again (i.e., recidivate at some level—arrest or prison). It is possible to calculate the cost of relapse on the criminal justice system. Given that the cost of housing an individual may exceed the cost of a drug treatment program in a correctional institution, it seems to indicate that the financial benefits of drug treatment exceed its costs.

The Heart of Cost-benefit Analysis

Cost-benefit analysis identifies and places monetary values on the costs of programs and weighing these against the benefits of the programs. A general formula for performing a cost-benefit analysis is to subtract costs from benefits to obtain the net benefits of a program. When the result is negative, this is referred to as net costs.

Lauria (2007) examined the cost-benefit utility of an assigned vehicle program (AVP). The crux of the study was to determine if the benefits of the AVP outweighed the cost of the program. The analysis showed that the benefits of assigning vehicles and allowing them to be taken home far outweighed the cost. Allowing officers to take their vehicles home improved police productivity and freed up additional

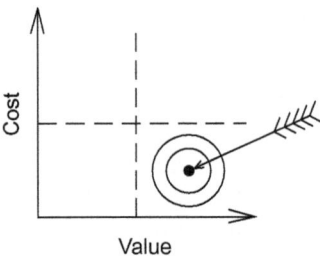

Figure 7.1 An ideal result of a cost-benefit analysis would be low cost for relatively high value.

municipal funds because secure parking was not needed. See Figure 7.1 for an example.

The Heart of Cost-effectiveness Analysis

Cost-effectiveness analysis seeks to identify and place dollars on the cost of the program (Levin, 1983). In cost-effectiveness analysis, the evaluator links the cost of a program to specific measures of program effectiveness. Generally, a cost-effectiveness ratio provides the information for the analysis. An example of this general ratio is:

$$\text{cost-effectiveness ratio} = \text{total cost}/\text{units of effectiveness}$$

The unit of effectiveness is the quantifiable outcome mentioned earlier. For instance, a drug treatment program may consider the number of days that someone is sober. Using the preceding formula, dividing the costs by the number of days the individual is sober, the evaluator is able to interpret the cost ratio as "dollars per days sober." This has an advantage of allowing the cost-effective ratio of more than one drug treatment program to be compared to determine which policy costs less per unit of effectiveness.

One issue to keep in mind is that the evaluator may be able to compute multiple cost-effectiveness ratios of interest. This means that the evaluator may evaluate different parts of a program to determine if they are cost effective. It could be that the overall program may not be cost effective, but parts of the program work well and are cost effective. The evaluator may be able to use this information in his or her recommendations. The opposite is also possible. The evaluator may discover that certain parts of the program are not cost effective, and then recommend that those parts of the program be eliminated or revised.

One example of cost-effectiveness analysis comes from Craddock's (2004) evaluation of a day reporting center (DRC). DRCs are a community-based offender program that offers the following goals:

- Increased surveillance.

- Provide treatment.
- Focus on confined offenders.

DRCs have the potential to reduce the prison or jail population. Using a single location, most DRCs have the same structure:

1. The offender is to report to the center regularly and frequently.
2. There is an increased number of contacts per week through this system.
3. The offender receives services not available in an intensive manner.

The goals and structure may force DRCs to have costs that differ from other forms of community corrections.

Craddock (2004) compared two DRCs within the same state, one rural and one urban. The rural DRC services a population of offenders who are chosen to go through the program before additional offenses occur. In the urban area, DRC is an alternative to probation revocation because offenders were displaying violation behavior. Craddock's results show that the rural DRC is better at reducing the likelihood for recidivism, but the urban DRC did not reduce recidivism.

These two outcomes have important implications for cost effectiveness. On one hand, the DRC in the rural area shows a cost savings because the offenders did not recidivate as much. On the other hand, the urban area shows a loss to the system because offenders did recidivate. The urban area result is logical considering the higher recidivism of these offenders. It is important to keep in mind that the criteria for participation in the DRC are different for these two locations. Overall, the results of the DRC evaluation show that one was more cost effective than the other.

Issues of Cost Analyses

A cost analysis requires the inspection of a number of issues. These issues are no more or less important than the issues discussed up to this point. The relevance of these issues is that they may influence the perception and reception of the cost analysis. It is important to understand that there is not a standard way of handling these issues, and these issues will change in importance and relevance for each evaluation or plan for a program.

Unit of Analysis

The unit of analysis is an important feature to keep in mind. Babbie (2002) discusses units of analysis as the things used to create summary descriptions of all such units and explain differences among them. Evaluators and planners use units of analysis to make observations. The same thing occurs in cost analyses. Evaluators and planners have to establish the unit of analysis, which should be compatible with the goals of the program. For instance, if the goal of a program is to change an individual's attitudes about crime and deviance, but the cost figures of the program are at the community level. The goals of the program and the unit of analysis are not the same. This will not result in accurate cost analysis for this particular program. To fix this issue, the cost figures should be at the individual level rather than the community level.

Establishing a unit of analysis is not always an easy task. The unit of analysis may change within an evaluation or for different evaluations. The unit of analysis for a community corrections program will be different than the unit of analysis for a policing hot-spots program. While both may have an end result that benefits society, their unit of analyses to determine the benefit will be different.

Stakeholders who are involved in the evaluation or planning of a program may have direct or indirect influence as to the unit of analysis. On one hand, stakeholders may have the ability to make some data available or withhold some data. Further, some stakeholders may have direct experience in the area that may be able to shape the determination of the unit of analysis for the cost analysis. On the other hand, stakeholders may have an indirect effect by shaping goals and objectives of the programs. Goals and objectives are useful in determining the unit of analysis for an evaluation.

The impact of a program does not always have to be linear. Consider the following linear relationship: more time in drug treatment reduces the likelihood of relapse. This type of linear relationship is unlikely. Someone who spends more time in drug treatment may require additional drug treatment upon release from initial stay, employment, or residence in a new area. In other words, these other factors serve as interactions with drug treatment that reduces the likelihood of relapse

What Do Future Costs and Benefits Hold?

The future brings about changes in program clients, missions, goals, or objectives. This means that cost and benefits will change in the future as well. Because these changes will occur, the evaluator or planner needs to think about and provide evidence of the benefits that can be expected in the future. For instance, an individual who successfully completes a drug rehabilitation program may be a more productive citizen (e.g., employed and have better physical health). While this is important, these long-term benefits are difficult to estimate.

The difficulty in estimating these long-term benefits becomes complex when considering the externality effect. The externality effect is known as a spillover. A spillover occurs when more benefits are realized from a program than those that are initially intended. For instance, the individual who successfully completed drug rehabilitation may also commit less criminal activity. This could mean more funds for a community because fewer funds could be necessary for the criminal justice system. Further, when criminal activity goes down, business and industry may move in to an area and, if on a grand enough scale, revitalize the area. While this is an important externality, quantifying the possibility of less criminal activity is not direct, nor is it an easy task.

The difficulty for this process comes from the timing of the funds. Different funds are necessary at the time a potential program or operating program is occurring than in the future. For instance, the amount of funds that are necessary for a program today may be insufficient to operate the program two years from now. The benefits also suffer in the same way—that is, the benefit is worth less two years later. Knowing the funds necessary to operate the program and the benefit from the program are important to make sure that a complete examination of the alternatives may take place.

Formally, discounting refers to the calculation of future benefit. The process is complex for noneconomists. A way of understanding discounting is for the evaluator or the planner to consider the rate of return. The rate of return is the amount the benefit will return from expending the funds. Practically, the rate of return is a percentage that is attached to the benefit. Because this is a future benefit and the desire is to have an accurate discount, evaluators should consult the empirical research literature and use experience to arrive at a realistic rate of return. When experience is not present, interviewing those who have experience is paramount. The rate-of-return percentage allows for the calculation of the discount. Evaluators have to compare the discount of one potential program to another to determine if the opportunity costs exceed the benefit.

Paying Costs and Reaping Benefits

The focus to this point has been about paying costs and reaping benefits. An immediate view is that those who pay the cost will reap the benefits. The costs of policing are covered by the community, but only those who call directly on the police may benefit. The other residents of the community may only indirectly benefit from the police. When the community is deemed safe, more people may move to the community, which may increase the tax base that could attract other programming (e.g., better schools) to sustain the community growth.

Using Cost-benefit and Cost-effectiveness Analysis

When the costs and benefits are priced in dollars, a cost-benefit analysis can be done. Decisions can be made based on the cost-benefit analysis. This makes it clear that supporting or not supporting a program involves more than a positive impact or outcome evaluation. Further, the limitations that come from budgets hinder the ability of those working in criminal justice organizations from making free decisions. This means that a cost-benefit analysis that shows a program is worthy of funds but exceeds the organization's budget is not feasible, but it pushes the organization to make decisions using the available resources. In other words, the best program may not be the most efficient or feasible.

When more than one program is expressed in different units, relating cost to outcomes is still important. While direct comparisons are not feasible, putting the options next to one another provide the opportunity for debate and transparency. Being able to see the options allows evaluators or planners the opportunity to examine financial limits and goals of their organization to help decision makers understand the potential impact of their choices.

Limits of Cost Analyses

Cost analyses have a number of limits. These limits tend to result in criticisms. The criticisms are generally unwarranted because it is important to understand the potential or actual cost of a program before embarking on the venture. With this in mind, the evaluator or planner has to keep in mind these limits and work vigilantly to address them. Further, the evaluator or planner has to make an effort to demonstrate his or her consideration of these limits.

Value of Life

When asked, many will say that they are uncomfortable placing a dollar figure on an individual's life. One of the methods of placing a value on life is through earning potential. The earning potential focus has some limits. First, earning potential does not take into account the amount of money spent on children as they develop. Second, earning potential will not properly estimate the value of an elderly individual. These two issues illuminate that earning potential is likely to miss large portions of society.

Even with these issues, some evaluations require that a value be placed on life. Evaluators use the additional earnings required to employ individuals in jobs where injury or accidental deaths are higher than most jobs and the difference that people are willing to pay to reduce a risk. For instance, sworn officers may receive hazardous duty pay, which is higher than nonsworn employees (e.g., dispatchers) of a police department. While this example may seem clear, most distinctions between injurious and accidental death jobs and noninjurious or nonaccidental death jobs are not as clear.

Assumptions and Cost Analysis

A complete cost analysis (either cost-benefit or cost-effectiveness analysis) requires that evaluators make a number of assumptions. To date, no minimum standards are present to guide evaluators in selecting assumptions; thus, evaluators may make a number of approximations that render a cost analysis as supporting a predetermined opinion. Evaluators have to be open and honest about their assumptions and approximations. This allows for the best examination of the validity of the analyses. Consider an evaluator who uses multiple discount rates or different assumptions to evaluate a program, but the evaluator still arrives at the same conclusions, so the confidence in the program increases.

An important issue for evaluators is to provide multiple estimates for cost-benefit and cost-effective analyses. Evaluators should use different methods to create a range of estimates for these types of analyses. The different methods should be balanced, where some of the assumptions favor the program, but others are not as supportive of the program. If the program remains cost effective no matter the methods or assumptions, the program gains credibility. If the program can only be shown to be effective under certain conditions, the program is tenuous at best.

Summary

Understanding cost is a necessary part of the operation of an organization in the criminal justice environment. Evaluators who use cost-analysis techniques are able to better inform criminal justice organizations with program selection and management of current programs. When the benefits of a program can be converted into dollars, a cost-benefit analysis can be performed. Even when this cannot be done, cost can be used as an organizing tool to compare to learn which program is more efficient, placing an emphasis on evaluating outcomes in light of the costs.

Discussion Questions

1. Identify a program from the criminal justice field. Prepare to perform a cost-effectiveness evaluation. Discuss the program outcomes for this program. What are the choices for the outcomes?
2. Discuss whether it is more important to know a program's cost or its effectiveness.

3. Discuss whether the following outcomes are likely to be monetary or nonmonetary. Would your evaluation be a cost-benefit or a cost-effectiveness study?
   a. Increased staff motivation in a correctional setting.
   b. Reduced alcohol and drug use among inmates.
   c. Reduced anxiety for police officers.
   d. Improved court participant satisfaction.
4. A potentially successful treatment program has a long waiting list of potential clients. As the new manager, what actions could you take to reduce the waiting list? Make a list of these and discuss each relative to a cost-benefit analysis.

References

Babbie, E. (2002). *The basics of social research* (2nd ed.). Belmont, CA: Wadsworth.

Craddock, A. (2004). Estimating criminal justice system costs and cost-savings benefits of day reporting centers. *Journal of Offender Rehabilitation, 39,* 69–98.

Lauria, D. T. (2007). Cost-benefit analysis of tacoma's assigned vehicle program. *Police Quarterly, 10,* 192–217.

Levin, H. M. (1983). *Cost-effectiveness, a primer: New perspectives in evaluation* (Vol. 4). Newbury Park, CA: Sage.

Royse, D., & Thyer, B. A. (1996). *Program evaluation: An introduction.* Chicago: Nelson-Hall, Inc.

Thompson, M. S. (1980). *Benefit-cost analysis for program evaluation.* Thousand Oaks, CA: Sage.

MEASUREMENT AND DATA ANALYSIS

Keywords

conceptualization
operational definition
mean
median
mode
variance
standard deviation

CHAPTER OUTLINE
Introduction   111
Measurement   112
    Construction of the Item   112
    Measurement Levels   115
    Validity and Reliability   116
Statistics   117
    Descriptive Statistics   118
        Graphical Displays   119
    Inferential Statistics   121
        Logic of Inferential Statistics   121
        Statistical Tools   123
Summary   126
Discussion Questions   126
References   126

Introduction

The major question facing an evaluator is: How do I get the proper data to examine my hypotheses or to answer my question? The second question facing an evaluator is: How do I analyze the data when I get them? Up to this point, a number of issues facing the evaluator have been discussed, and they include different forms of evaluation (i.e., needs, process, outcomes, and theory-driven), evaluation designs (i.e., experimental, quasi-experimental, survey, and qualitative), reliability, and validity issues (i.e., internal and external). For each one of these issues, the process is still the same: clearly define the problem that needs to be evaluated. If the evaluation is to determine the effectiveness of a program, the evaluator will need to plan precisely how he or she is going to go about this task. A few issues to keep in mind are that the data necessary to perform an evaluation may not be readily available. This means that the evaluator may have to rely on secondary data, which are data not originally collected by the evaluator (e.g., government reports or agency data). Data that the evaluator collects are known as primary data. No matter the data type, some information will be lost through the measurement process.

Once the data are obtained, the evaluator then has to make sense of the data through analysis. Unless using qualitative methods, the evaluator will likely use statistics. Statistics are a set of tools that evaluators can use to make decisions with limited information. Statistics provide the evaluator with methods for organization or summarization. This chapter is divided into two broad sections: the first deals with the measurement process for primary and secondary data, and the second deals with the statistical tools necessary to perform an analysis in an evaluation.

Measurement

Because qualitative methods have been covered in Chapter 5, the emphasis of measurement in this chapter will be on quantification. The evaluator should think about quantification in everyday terms. For instance, the speed of a car, intelligence, or people who have been reached by a program may be quantified. In criminal justice, a substantial amount of information is collected on crime, mental health, drug use, or violence. For an evaluator, the essence of measurement is to assign a number to properties or attributes using specific rules (Eck, 2010). The rules of measurement focus on the construction and operationalization of the item.

Construction of the Item

Constructing an item can occur using several steps regardless if the data are primary or secondary. The process is still the same, but with secondary data, most of this has already been completed; thus, the construction of an item is generally thought to be for primary data. At this point, it is instructive to understand that the construction of the item is the development of the statement or the question, but not the use of answer choices. Understanding that a concept is an abstraction from reality that cannot be seen, but it is present, is important. For instance, rehabilitation is a concept that drug abuse evaluators consistently use. It is not possible to see rehabilitation, but it should be defined in terms of the program being evaluated or program theory. To assist the evaluator, conceptualization is a process that may be carried out in a number of steps.

First, the evaluator has to conceptualize all of the items for the evaluation. Conceptualization is the process of specifying the meaning of the terms in the evaluation (Nunnally & Bernstein, 1994). For example, the evaluator wants to know whether a program successfully rehabilitates methamphetamine addicts. In communication with program administration or staff, the evaluator has to develop a working agreed-on meaning of rehabilitates or rehabilitation to move forward with the evaluation. The agreement that the definition is the best is not necessary. Overall, this part of the process provides an agreed-on definition for evaluation purposes.

Second, once the conceptualization is in place, the evaluator has to search for indicators. An indicator signals the presence or absence of the concept being studied. The evaluator has to understand the type of evaluation that is being performed. A needs, process, outcome, or theory-driven evaluation may require different definitions of the same concept. Going back to the rehabilitation example, an evaluator may define it as something that is necessary to revive a community in a needs evaluation, but in a process evaluation, the evaluator may deem it as the type and amount of services that are being provided. In an outcome evaluation, the evaluator may define it as the number of days, months, or years being sober. Overall, the type of evaluation matters. Table 8.1 shows that the type of conceptualization and indicators differ for the types of evaluation.

Table 8.1 Types of Evaluation and Indicators

Type of Evaluation	Indicator
Needs	Social indicators to help outline the need to be addressed (e.g., burglary rates)
Process	Indicators of implementation
Impact	Indicators of success or failure of the program
Theory-driven	Indicators of the theory

At this point, the evaluator may think of multiple things to measure. For instance, he or she may use the program theory and goals, missions, or objectives to conceptualize the program outcome. When this is the case, the program goals have to be specific. In criminal justice, the program goals, mission, or objectives revolve around a few things: effects on people (i.e., treatment, education, employment, etc.), effects on agencies (e.g., improve skills of staff, make organization work better, etc.), or effects on the public (e.g., more police officers in an area to reduce crime rates).

In addition, the program processes are important to measure, depending on the type of evaluation. An evaluator may easily be able to measure elements of implementation that are important to process evaluations, such as characteristics of staff, duration of service, stability of activity, or quality of service.

Next, program inputs, resources, and the environment are possible concepts that may be used as outcomes for an evaluation. These are things that go into a program (e.g., budget, staff with proper credentials, physical site, number of physical sites, or plan of activities). All inputs do not have to come from the organization. Some inputs come from the participants, including age, gender, income, race/ethnicity, language, attitudes, motivations for participation, or expectations of the program.

Third, the evaluator needs to consult with others and the empirical literature. This provides the evaluator with additional focus and clarification of the concepts. If the evaluator has completed other parts of the evaluation process (e.g., theory-driven evaluation), the consultation with others will provide some indication of what the measures should be for the evaluation. The use of this information will highlight disagreements about the definition of concepts. Rehabilitation may mean different things to program staff and evaluators in other fields.

Fourth, the disagreement should reveal different parts or pieces of a concept, called dimensions. To clarify, dimensions are a specifiable part of a concept that may be quantified. For instance, methamphetamine rehabilitation may consist of methadone treatments, counseling, and residential stay. Therefore, a concept should be able to be subdivided into quantifiable parts (DeVellis, 1991). In other words, conceptualization includes specifying dimensions and indicators for each.

The evaluator should keep in mind that the specification of the dimensions of a concept will lead to a better understanding through the evaluation process. For instance, an evaluator may be evaluating the effectiveness of a program on truancy. The evaluator is not able to determine the effectiveness without the proper identification of the dimensions; thus, conceptualization is an important tool that all evaluators must use.

Fifth, the evaluator is able to put all of this information into a single or multiple items, known as operational definitions. The operational definition is the actual statement or questions that are designed to capture information about the dimensions or indicators. While some disagreement may be present about the conceptualization (i.e., conceptual definition), a working definition is possible and necessary to use. The development of operational definitions provides a clear statement or question for a respondent (i.e., someone to address).

Sixth, the evaluator needs to choose a measurement level, if possible, to capture the information from the operational definition. The measurement level relates how the operational definitions are scaled for use. Specifically, the measurement level links the operational definition to a method of assigning numbers to them. This process is important because measurement level has major implications for the type of statistical analysis that is possible. While this is the sixth issue in the construction of an item, the determination of the measurement level is central to a measure.

Measurement Levels

The first measurement level is the nominal level. This is the lowest level of measurement. For nominal data, the numbers classify the characteristics of the operational definition. For example, gender is, generally, captured using male or female. This shows that the nominal level of measurement provides names or labels for characteristics. The evaluator has to keep in mind that nominal-level data have the property of equivalence, which means that neither males nor females are ranked higher than another.

The measurement level is ordinal. Ordinal-level data allow an evaluator to name the characteristics or attributes but also provide some rank order. In other words, the evaluator is able to group data in a way to tell if some data contain more or less. Examples of ordinal-level data are social class or political affiliation. An evaluator using social class may be able to group data in a way that some groups have or may earn more money than others. For instance, the evaluator may categorize income earnings in the past year as data for social class as: (a) $0–10,000, (b) $10,001–50,000, (c) $50,001–100,000, and (d) $100,001 and higher. Obviously, these categories are crude and may be expanded for greater detail, but they demonstrate that placing someone in one of these categories will suggest that they either earn more or less money in a year.

The third measurement level is the interval level. This scale has all of the attributes of the ordinal level. In addition, the distance between any two numbers (i.e., the interval) on the scale is a known size. The interval scale is not only known but it is constant where real numbers are assigned to each interval. Assigning numbers to these intervals allows the evaluator to count the distance between the observations. An evaluator who is interested in a policing program to reduce burglaries after 9:00 p.m. will note the time that each burglary has taken place. The difference between the times is the interval.

The fourth measurement level is the ratio level. This level of measurement has all of the attributes of interval level, but it also has a true zero point. The zero point allows the evaluator to calculate and state the ratio between any two values on a scale. Think of the number of new arrests. An individual may have no new arrests or several new arrests.

Once the evaluator has this information, he or she has to determine whether to measure over a short-term or long-term time period. The issue with this decision influences the wording of the operational definition, and it may influence the manner that the measurement levels are applied to the operational definition. For instance, an item to capture a drug rehabilitation program outcome could be: Was the individual sober for 30 days? The information may be captured using nominal-level data. However, if the item was written for how many years the individual has been sober, the measurement level may be better written at the ordinal level. This means that the evaluator is grouping together the number of years. However, the number of years may also be used as ratio-level data. This should make it clear that short-term or long-term information makes a difference in the construction of an item and the measurement level.

Generally, a single item is not capable of capturing the entire content of the domain (i.e., the spread of the conceptual dimensions) for a concept, no matter the measurement level; thus, multiple items are necessary. The compilation of multiple items generally results in some form of a survey, checklist, or test. A survey is a document—paper and pencil or electronic—that contains multiple items that can capture sensitive information (Babbie, 2002). The measurement level is unrestricted in a survey. A checklist is much like a survey, but it is restricted to a nominal measurement level. A test is also similar to a survey, but it is used primarily in an educational format.

Validity and Reliability

Using multiple items allows the evaluator to examine important properties of the items—namely, validity and reliability. Validity is the determination of whether the items are behaving in the manner that they should be behaving. For instance, a measure of self-control should capture self-control and not peer association. Validity has multiple forms, but three forms are relevant for the evaluator: content, face, and construct.

Content validity is concerned if the evaluator's measure is capturing the entire content of domain or dimensions of a concept (Babbie, 2002). For instance, when testing criminal behavior, the measure cannot be restricted to burglary; it needs to include all facets of criminal behavior. Face validity is concerned about whether measures are consistent with common agreements or images of a concept. For instance, the face validity of a measure of self-control may come into question. Some items that go in to creating a measure of self-control may resemble other concepts (e.g., sensation seeking). The issue here is that on its "face" the items may not be completely about self-control. Construct validity is concerned with the relationships among the variables (Babbie, 2002). For instance, a theoretical concept (e.g., self-control) has an expected relationship with behavior (e.g., crime). The expected relationship is that as self-control decreases, crime increases. If the data show this, then construct validity is present.

Reliability is also a concern. Reliability has to do with the consistency of the items (DeVellis, 1991). n other words, over time, do the items provide the same result? When the evaluator has validity and reliability of the measures, he or she is able to proceed to statistical tools for more analysis.

Statistics

With the construction of an item complete, the evaluator has to choose the proper statistical tool for proper analysis because he or she now possesses quantified data. Due to time and money, evaluators will examine attributes from a sample of the population that comes in a way that is representative of the entire population. When the evaluator does this properly, he or she is able to make inferences based on the data collected and from the sample. A representative sample of the population means that the data are collected in a manner where the data are normal.

Normally distributed data means that they may be graphically presented as a bell curve. In essence, the term *normal* is making reference to the type of curve and distribution having certain properties. The evaluator has to become comfortable because of issues outside of their control; thus, their data may not resemble a bell curve. Their data may be asymmetric or elongated in either end of the tail of the distribution, known as skewness. When the curve is elongated to the right, the data are negatively skewed, and when the curve is elongated to the left, is the data are positively skewed. In addition to skewed data, the evaluator may have to use data that have sharp peaks, known as kurtosis. The data type will suggest to the evaluator the types of statistical tools that are appropriate.

Before this selection is to take place, the evaluator has to remember that statistics are not "magical," or come with all of the answers, but that statistics are tools that provide information to aid decision making. Evaluators have to keep in mind that the statistical tools are only as useful as the quality of their data.

With this in mind, the evaluator needs to begin making decisions about using the proper statistical tools and remembering the assumptions that come with each statistical tool. This section will cover descriptive and inferential statistics. In addition, this section will provide some criteria for selecting the proper statistical test. While a complete review of all assumptions and issues concerning statistical tools would be ideal, many books properly cover the topic.

Descriptive Statistics

In situations where an evaluation requires counting, the evaluator is to follow certain procedures. The procedures organize and make the count data understandable. The evaluator is able to describe the characteristics of the data so they can be comprehended. These statistical tools provide a concise description of the centrality and distribution of the data. The most common forms of descriptive statistics are mean, median, mode, variance, and standard deviation.

The *mean* is the most popular form of descriptive statistic as it is the average score in the distribution (Blalock, 1979). This is the score that comes from adding the scores in a set of data and then dividing this sum by the total score. This results in comparing the sum of scores into a per-element format; thus, the evaluator may compare the average across different groups. Evaluators may use the mean with any measurement level. The evaluator has to keep in mind that the mean provides a percentage when using nominal-level data. For instance, if an evaluator captures gender as male = 1 and female = 0 and they have a mean of 0.4, after multiplying 0.4 × 100, the evaluator should interpret this as 40% of the sample is male. The mean does have problems—it is sensitive to extreme scores or outliers.

The *mode* (Blalock, 1979) is the number in the data that occurs most frequently. No statistical computation is necessary, and the evaluator simply observes the number that occurs the most by reading the frequency distribution. The evaluator needs to keep in mind that a data distribution may have more than one mode, known as multimodal. The mode may occur no matter the measurement level, and it may come at any point in the distribution. Because the mode is not a form of statistical computation, it is not able to be used in any further statistical analysis.

The *median* (Blalock, 1979) is the midpoint or middle of the data distribution. To clarify, this is the point in the data where 50% of the scores are above or below, dividing the distribution into equal halves. Because the median is the midpoint, a data distribution may have only one median. The median requires at least ordinal-level data and it is not influenced by extreme scores.

Other descriptive statistics are classified as measures of variability. Here, two measures of variability are relevant for the evaluator. If all of the values in a data distribution were the same, the evaluator would not need statistics. Because this is unlikely, the evaluator needs to be able to gain an appreciation for the amount of dispersion in the data. An accounting of the dispersion in data comes from the measure of variability. The two most prominent measures of variability for an evaluator are the variance and standard deviation.

The *variance* is the mean of the sum of all squared deviations from the mean of any distribution of scores (Blalock, 1979). In other words, the variance is the amount of squared deviations of the mean. The evaluator can easily find the variance by performing the following number of steps:

1. Calculate the mean.
2. Find the deviation from the mean. This is calculated by subtracting the mean from each number in the distribution.
3. Square each solution in step 2.
4. Calculate the mean in step 3. This is the average squared deviation from the mean or the variance.

Often, the variance provides numbers that do not make sense. The standard deviation provides a method to fix this problem. The *standard deviation* is the square root of the variance (Blalock, 1979). This becomes the single number that is representative of the deviations from the mean found in the data distribution. The standard deviation is important for data that are at least ordinal. The importance of the standard deviation for the evaluator is that it provides information on the type of deviation from the mean. With a normal distribution, two-thirds of the distribution should be within one standard deviation of the mean.

Descriptive statistics provide a wealth of information. Using a combination of these forms of descriptive statistics, the evaluator is able to provide a clear picture of the data in the report. In many instances, the use of the mean and standard deviation are the main two descriptive statistics that the evaluator needs to use.

Graphical Displays

One of the best methods of providing a clear picture is to present descriptive statistics using graphs. Graphs provide a number of desirable features: visibility of data, some indication of the meaning of the data, rapid and simple interpretation, and plotting the frequencies and descriptive statistics.

For instance, a pie chart provides a simple example. A pie chart provides a picture of a 360-degree circle that represents the percentages of the data (Vito et al., 2008). The evaluator is able to visually

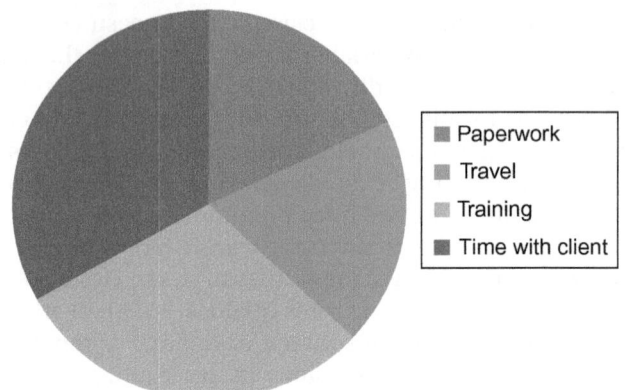

Figure 8.1 Pie chart example of time allocation of a program.

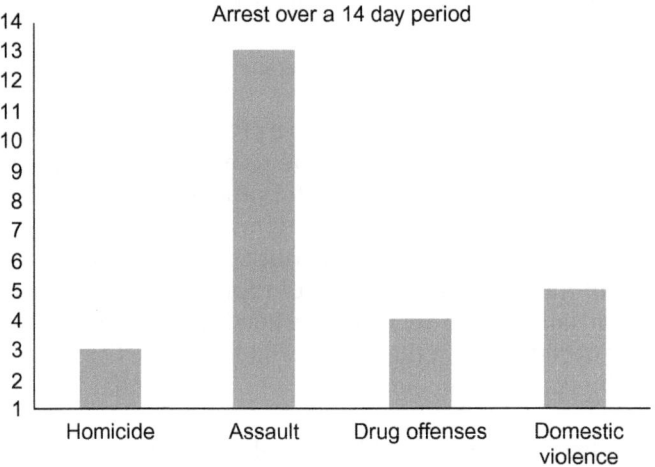

Figure 8.2 Bar chart example of arrest types for a 14-day period.

compare the size of the various segments of the data. In Figure 8.1, the different pieces represent different percentages of time allocation of a program. This may be a useful feature of a process evaluation to help with efficiency.

Another important form of graphing that the evaluator may be able to use is a bar chart. A bar chart is used to represent nominal-level and ordinal-level of data. Bar charts allow an evaluator to describe categorical data with bars that are separated by spaces, and the height of the bars represents the frequencies or percentages so the evaluator can make comparisons (Vito et al., 2008). Figure 8.2 shows a bar chart for arrest types that have occurred in a location over a 14-day period.

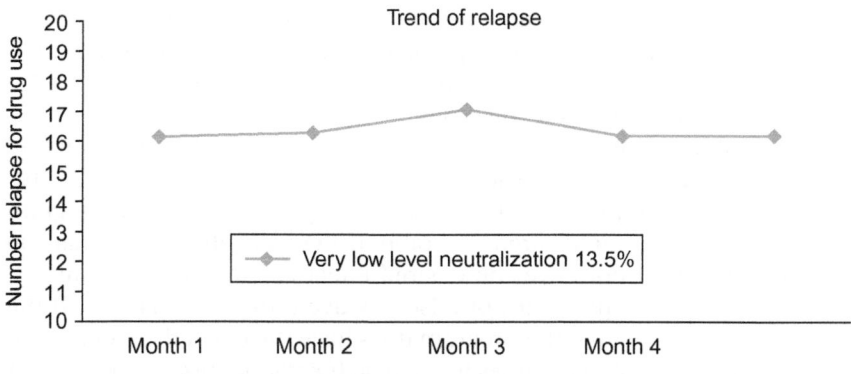

Figure 8.3 Line graph example for trend of relapse.

In addition, a line graph may be used to represent data. This graph type is ideal for trend data (Vito et al., 2008). Essentially, a line graph describes numerical data with a dot where each attribute represents the frequency or mean. The dots are then connected by a line to highlight the different values. In the line graph, the frequencies or means are plotted on the vertical axis and the values for the attributes are placed on the horizontal axis. For example, an evaluator is examining the months of relapse after 300 individuals completed the same drug treatment program. To illustrate the effectiveness, the evaluator presents the number of relapses by month as shown in Figure 8.3. The line graph shows the trends of relapse, but the goals of the program have to be considered to determine the quality of the trends.

Once the evaluator has completed the descriptive statistics, he or she should use some form of graphing to provide a clear picture of the data. This will assist the evaluator and the consumer of the evaluation in understanding the data better.

Inferential Statistics

Once the descriptive statistics show the data, the evaluator needs to consider greater implications. These implications come from inferential statistics. This section has two parts: logic of inferential statistics and statistical tools. Understanding the logic of inferential statistics is important to understanding the results of the statistical tools.

Logic of Inferential Statistics

Applying inferential statistics requires a systematic procedure known has hypothesis testing. A statistical hypothesis identifies the link between any two variables of interest. These procedures include the statement of the null hypothesis. A null hypothesis in program evaluation may be that the program does not have an effect on achieving the intended outcome.

Problems come about when there is a difference between the true situation and the test results. In a residential drug treatment situation, for example, a poor conclusion may be drawn if the program does not have the desired outcome. If the true situation is that the program does not have the desired effect but the statistics suggest that it does, a type I error or false-positive error has occurred. If the true situation is that the program does have the desired effect but the test data suggest that it does not, a type II error or false-negative error has occurred.

The evaluator has to recognize that it is difficult to guard against both types of errors, so he or she has to consider the cost of each type of error while focusing on avoiding the most costly of the two. Consider that a false positive may be more costly than a false negative. For example, an evaluator may find that a very costly drunk-driving prevention program is effective when it really is not, thereby resulting in a substantial amount of unnecessary funding. A false-negative conclusion that an effective measure for reducing disproportionate minority contact (DMC) is not working may mean that the measure is not used anymore, erroneously resulting in an increase in DMC. An evaluators has to weigh the consequences of committing both false-positive and false-negative errors. After weighing these consequences, the evaluator has to identify ways to reduce instances that minimize the most costly error. Once this is complete, the evaluator is able to develop rules to minimize the costs.

One way to do this is to adopt a rule such as the 95% rule. This is the amount of evidence evaluators may want to have to ensure that they are correct when they conclude that a program produces its desired effect. If the results from the data depart from what the probability tables predict if the null is true, the null hypothesis is rejected. This means that the results allow one to generalize the program effects in the sample to the population with the confidence that over the long run the test should result in a false-positive error (i.e., type I error) 5 times out of 100.

This is the essence of statistical significance. The link between two variables is statistically significant informs the audience that the link is real in the population from the sample. However, generalizing this link from the sample to the population must be done with caution. The evaluator has to keep in mind the threats to internal and external validity (see Chapter 6).

While statistical significance is an important feature to the generalizability of the results from a sample to a population, the evaluator needs to also consider practical significance, which is the consideration of the size of the effect. At this point, it is important to clarify that statistical significance and practical significance are two separate decisions—whether the sample data can be generalized (i.e., statistical significance) and evaluation of the size of the effect (i.e., practical significance). For example, if a new speed-trap program has been employed by law enforcement appears to raise the number of traffic citations by 1%, even if the large sample indicates that the effect is statistically significant, the size of the impact may be small. The problem with practical significance is that no standards are uniform for all situations, but this does not diminish or eliminate its importance. Evaluators need to gather information about the program to determine practical significance. For instance, an effect for one program may be small, but the same effect may be large for a different program depending on the program's goals, location, staff, and a number of other factors.

Statistical Tools

With these factors of inferential statistics, a number of statistical tools may be used to provide information that the evaluator may use for an understanding of statistical significance and practical significance. In this presentation of the statistical tools, we avoid the use of statistical formulas and provide a conceptual presentation of the statistical tools because we assume that the evaluator will have access to some form of statistical package (e.g., excel, SPSS, SAS, or STATA) to perform these tests. The tools are t-test, chi-square, correlation, and regression.

t-Test

The t-test, developed by W. S. Gossett in 1908, is a statistical tool that can handle small and large data sets. The distribution is designed for sample data. Evaluators use the t-test when there are two groups (e.g., pre-test and post-test groups). T-tests are able to compare the differences between two groups. The t-test requires that quantitative data be measured at the interval level (e.g., age, weight, test scores, scale scores), but also a grouping variable be measured at the nominal level (e.g., pre-test and post-test). Evaluators use the t-test when they are not able to randomly assign into pre-test and post-test groups. While there are different forms of t-tests, the evaluator who is using data that are not randomly assigned would use an independent samples t-test.

The use of the t-test distribution, which is similar to a normal distribution, allows for the development of hypotheses and significance tests (i.e., statistical and practical) (Blalock, 1979). The evaluator has to keep in mind that the distribution is symmetrical. The symmetry of the distribution shows that it has a mean of zero, and the exact position of t-statistic is determined by degrees of freedom.

Vito, Tewksbury & Higgins (2010) performed an evaluation of an early release program in the state of Kentucky. The premise of the program was to move offenders back to the community before the expiration of their sentence. The purpose of the evaluation was to determine if these offenders posed a creditable threat to public safety. We used data from those individuals who were released early and matched the comparison group. Note that the matched comparison group was based on the characteristics of the released group. To determine if the released group and the comparison group were similar, Vito & colleagues (2010) use the t-test as one technique. Specifically, they examined whether the two groups differed by age and days served. They showed that the released and comparison groups did not differ by age, but their t-test showed that the released group and comparison group did differ by number of days served. The information from this part of the analysis led Vito & colleagues (2010) to argue that their comparison does approximate the released group.

Chi-square

Evaluators are consistently faced with the need to test for differences among three or more groups, or to compare two or more samples with nominal-level data. The chi-square statistical tool provides an approach for testing the significance between categorical levels of data (Blalock, 1979).

The chi-square test may be used when the objective is to determine whether a set of observed frequencies differs from those that are to be expected from theoretical assumptions. For instance, the evaluator may want know whether racial groups tend to benefit differently from job training programs. If a random sample is taken from the racial groups who received the job training program, the chi-square test can be used to determine whether the proportion of success differs across racial groups.

Importantly, the chi-square test may be generalized to any situation where the interest is in the link between two nominal-level variables. This does not mean that the chi-square test cannot be used with ordinal-level variables, and some evaluators use it in this manner.

To properly use the chi-square test, evaluators have to make sure that they have a sufficient sample size. This will guarantee that cell frequencies are not too small. Because the formula for chi-square places the expected value of cell frequency in the denominator, the chi-square value will be overestimated if the cell values are too small. This situation will result in a rejection of the null hypothesis. To avoid this issue, evaluators should make sure that they have more than five frequencies in each cell.

The evaluator should keep in mind that the chi-square test does not provide information about how strongly two variables are related to each other. In other words, it does not provide direct information to determine practical significance. Additional tests are necessary to obtain this type of information.

One common test for this is the phi coefficient. The phi coefficient is applied properly when the data are at the nominal level. Evaluators have to keep in mind that a significant chi-square value means that the phi coefficient is significant as well. The phi coefficient ranges from 0 to 1, where 0 means no link and 1 means a perfect link. Other tests, such as Cramer's V, may be used when the data are mixed between nominal and ordinal. Cramer's V also ranges from 0 to 1, with 0 meaning no link and 1 meaning a perfect link.

Remaining with the Vito et al. (2010) example, they used the chi-square test to determine if the released and comparison group differed by gender. They showed that the percentages of males and females were similar to one another. This information helped them to argue that the two groups for their study were similar.

Correlation

An evaluator may need to know the extent to which two or more variables are related to each other. This may be addressed by handling three other issues:
- Whether an association exists.
- The strength of the association.
- The nature of the relationship.

The statistical tool that may address all of these issues is a correlation. A correlation measures the degree that two or more variables are associated. Further, the correlation provides a measure of the strength of the association. A correlation ranges from -1 to 1 (i.e., a perfect correlation). It is important for an evaluator to remember that a correlation that is 0.75 and -0.75 are of the same size. Finally, the positive or negative sign indicates the nature of the relationship, but not the strength. A positive relationship occurs when two variables increase or decrease together. It is possible for two variables to be inversely related to one another. This means that as one variable increases another variable decreases.

There are two types of correlations that an evaluator may use. When the evaluator's data are all interval level and above, the evaluator should use Pearson's version of correlation. When the evaluator's data are ordinal, the evaluator should use a Spearman rank correlation coefficient. Keep in mind, both tests provide the same information: strength of association and direction (i.e., positive or negative).

Regression

Regression analysis is an extension of correlation. Regression provides the evaluator an opportunity to predict the outcome of a relationship with an interval-level dependent variable and one or more independent variables. Dependent variables—sometimes referred to with Y—are caused by other variables, and independent variables—sometimes referred to with X—cause the changes in the dependent variables. If a correlation is zero, the proper predictor is the mean. However, when the correlation is nonzero and is 1, the prediction is perfect. When the correlation is less than 1, it is less accurate and "regresses" to the mean. To clarify, if the evaluator plots the values when the correlation is 1, then all of the values fall on the regression line. The closer the correlation is to 1, the closer to the regression line the values will fall.

Summary

Understanding the conceptualization and the types of measurement are critical to performing an evaluation. When the conceptualization results in quantitative data, the evaluator is able to use statistical tools to perform descriptive and inferential tests. The combinations of these tools are able to provide the evaluator and the criminal justice organization vital information.

Discussion Questions

1. Discuss the steps of conceptualization.
2. Discuss the differences between the levels of data.
3. Discuss the differences between descriptive and inferential statistics.

References

Babbie, E. (2002). *The basics of social research* (2nd ed.). Belmont, CA: Wadsworth.

Blalock, H. M. (1979). *Social statistics*. New York: McGraw-Hill.

DeVellis, R. (1991). *Scale development: Theory and applications*. Newbury Park, CA: Sage.

Eck, J. E. (2010). *Assessing responses to problems: An introductory guide for police problem solvers*. Washington, DC: U.S. Department of Justice, Office of Community-Oriented Policing Services.

Nunnally, J., & Bernstein, I. (1994). *Psychometric theory* (3rd ed.). New York: McGraw-Hill.

Vito, G. F., Tewksbury, R., & Higgins, G. E. (2010). Evaluation of Kentucky's early inmate release initiative: sentence, commutations, public safety, and recidivism. *Federal Probation, 74*, 22–26.

9

REPORTING AND USING EVALUATIONS

Keywords

Operation CeaseFire
host organization
violence interrupters
hot spots

CHAPTER OUTLINE
Introduction 127
Review of Operation CeaseFire Chicago 128
   Abstract or Program Summary 128
   Presenting the Theory Supporting the Program 129
   Presenting the Process Evaluation 130
   Presenting the Impact Evaluation 135
Factors Influencing the Use of Program Evaluation Results 136
Summary 139
Discussion Questions 139
References 140

The best quality evaluation study whose report never leaves the shelf, that is, is never utilized, may as well never been undertaken.
          —Douglas S. Lipton (Lipton, 1992, p.176)

Introduction

Lipton is right. Evaluation research has a purpose—to examine the efficiency and effectiveness of criminal justice programs and policies in this case. If the final report is to serve this purpose, it must be read and its results must be clearly and specifically communicated. This is the final task facing the evaluation researcher. If this task is not completed well, the entire exercise fails. The information must be placed in the hands of those who can use it or poor policies will continue and promising programs will not be implemented elsewhere. Here, we offer some suggestions on how to ensure that a program evaluation is read and its findings are utilized.

Lipton (1992) shares more problems and solutions to overcome communication barriers between program evaluators and policy makers. Again, he suggests that program evaluators must write their reports for policy makers, not for each other. Therefore, the aim of the report must be to provide information and advice on what should be done and which alternatives are worth consideration. This method will match the perceptions of policy makers and legislators with an eye toward the political realities of the situation. Program evaluators must prepare reports with executive summaries (no more than two pages) that address policy recommendations clearly. The body of the report should "be presented like a table of contents with summarizing headlines" (Lipton, 1992, p.187). Tables and figures should be limited to no more than two variables and the numbers presented should be carefully calculated so that there are no mistakes between presentations. All technical and methodological materials, while relevant to academic publication, should be presented in an appendix. Focusing on relevant questions, key conclusions should be presented in bullet-point format that recommend the first steps that should be taken to promote action on the policy under consideration. It is most important that these first steps are politically feasible and realistic and not utopian in nature.

Let's examine an actual criminal justice research evaluation report to see how these issues are dealt with and presented.

Review of Operation CeaseFire Chicago

This portion of the chapter focuses on one evaluation report to identify its key components as an example of how to construct a program evaluation. The report is on Operation CeaseFire Chicago—a program designed to reduce gun violence by gang members (Skogan, Hartnett, Bump & Dubois, 2008). Here, we review how the report is constructed and how well it follows recommended aspects of program evaluation. Our aim is to present a review of a program report in terms of what it contains and how well it describes the operations and outcomes generated by the program under evaluation.

Abstract or Program Summary

As many authors have suggested, this report begins with an abstract or program summary that presents the purpose of the program, how the evaluation was conducted, and a summary of research findings. As Weiss (1998, p. 295) stresses:

> *Give the main findings up front. An evaluation report is not a mystery story where the reader is kept guessing until the denouement at the end. Neither is it an academic paper that begins with a history of the question, a review of the previous research, and a description of the methodology. In an evaluation report, the findings come first. That's what people want to know.*

Here, the authors of the CeaseFire evaluation stress that the program was theory-driven and based on a violence prevention model. The research determined that clients were at a high risk for violence as determined by a number of risk indicators. The impact evaluation determined that CeaseFire had an impact on both shootings and killings in the areas served by the program.

Presenting the Theory Supporting the Program

The program evaluator must identify and describe the theory that serves as the basis for the program and the expectation that it will have the desired impact. The evaluation must examine the assumptions that served as the foundations of the program and the reasons why it was expected to be effective. In the CeaseFire report, Chapter 1 presents the theory behind the program. CeaseFire called on clients to stop shooting and killing—a risk management approach aimed at harm reduction (Skogan et al., 2008, p. 1-1). It also describes the target population for the program. These clients met several risk criteria set by the program:
- They were between the ages of 16 and 25 years old.
- They had a prior history of offending and arrests.
- They were either gang members, had been in prison, or were recent victims of a shooting.
- They were involved in street drug markets.

The program theory is clearly presented and clarified in the first chapter. The program aimed at providing "on-the-spot" alternatives to street violence by increasing the perceived risks and costs of involvement in violence via a "pulling levers" strategy: street intervention, client outreach, clergy involvement, community mobilization, an educational campaign, and cooperation between police and prosecutors. Each of these interventions is defined and then presented in the words of the program staff. These elements are presented in a summary figure. Closely aligned to the levers were an attempt to change community norms toward violence as an acceptable dispute-solving mechanism. Therefore, supporting quotations from program staffers are presented in this first chapter.

The first chapter also describes how the program stakeholders were introduced to and enlisted to support the program evaluation. The reports that they filled out and reports generated are identified as crucial to the evaluation from the program's outset. Crime trend data on the beats served by the program were carefully collected. The site visits made by program evaluators and their purpose is outlined and described in detail.

Presenting the Process Evaluation

In the example, the process evaluation is covered in several chapters of the CeaseFire report. Chapter 2 focuses on the process evaluation, specifically the selection of program sites and partners for the program. Here, the emphasis is on how the host organization served as the basis for the implementation of the program. It is important for the program evaluator to describe how the program was implemented. Such information not only should be considered in terms of program effectiveness, but also because it can provide valuable information to other individuals seeking to implement (or replicate) similar programs.

Here, the program evaluator must clearly present and specify how (and whether) the program was implemented according to its original design. The program construction and delivery should be carefully described in detail. In the CeaseFire program, the host organization performed a number of valuable functions. It identified the target areas for the program (i.e., areas with high levels of violence) and selected a community organization to house the program. Once the sites were chosen, the host organization continued to provide technical assistance and training, helped them develop a comprehensive plan for violence reduction, monitored workload at the sites, and reviewed files to make certain that clients were being served. In addition, the host organization carried out monthly and weekly meetings for various committees at the sites (steering committees, violence prevention coordinators, and outreach staff). The program headquarters also provided valuable support functions for the sites, including providing information, guidance, and models of best practices; producing materials (signs, bumper stickers, and t-shirts); and securing and maintaining funding for the sites from the state and federal levels.

The program evaluator should provide a description of how the service was delivered, both successfully and unsuccessfully. This analysis reveals the internal workings of the program (the "black box" of program operations). Information on what worked, what did not, and what was unexpected in terms of service delivery can be used by program administrators to alter operations and inform outsiders of potential sources of effectiveness and pitfalls to be avoided if they attempt to implement similar programs. In terms of the example here, the level of violence was the key feature of site selection. Another major factor was the capacity and ability of the community in question to deliver the services designed to be provided by the program. The evaluation revealed that some communities actively sought to be a CeaseFire site and brought political pressure to bear. The host organization monitored implementation at each site and gave appropriate feedback concerning site operations as needed.

The process evaluation should also contain relevant descriptive information on program operations. Here, the evaluator provides descriptions of organizational structure at the sites, demographic breakdowns of the communities served by each program site, and the levels of violence at each site when the program need was identified. This information is presented for each site via tables and colorful maps.

The process evaluation should also consider the management of the program, particularly staffing and funding. In the CeaseFire report, Chapter 3 highlights how this process was conducted. Several staffing problems are identified, including dealing with the decentralized nature of the program and the special case of faith-based partners. Other problems are noted relating to the program's overall commitment to hiring high-risk community members to staff the program and issues ranging from conducting background checks, staff drug testing, and staff career development and turnover. The consideration of such issues is presented in the process evaluation because they have a significant effect on service delivery and program operations. They are crucial to the assessment of the program's ability to meet its original goals. It is especially significant in a program like CeaseFire where multiple program sites (30) were identified and selected.

The process evaluation should also describe and assess how the desired service was provided by the program. Here the nature of program management should be frankly described and assessed. Chapter 4 of the CeaseFire report explains how outreach workers identified and engaged with clients of the program—its target population. It describes how outreach workers were recruited and trained, and how they recruited clients and provided services to them. Accordingly, it also presents clients' background and describes how clients were recruited and served. One of the key features of hiring for outreach workers was their street-level credibility that would assist them in presenting a convincing message to their similarly situated clients. This background has its strengths and weaknesses. While street experience provided credibility to clients, it also was a source of temptation to outreach workers who might be tempted to be involved in both worlds—the street life and the program services.

This tendency provided a challenge to supervisors to determine when such a problem arose. One of their crucial tasks was preparing their clients for the real world of legitimate work. For the service to be truly provided, these workers had to establish a personal relationship with their clients. They also had to establish ties with community members, explaining the purpose of the program and canvassing them for support. The outreach workers also faced the challenge of transitioning their clients to a new lifestyle. Thus, they had to maintain a visible street presence to maintain contact with their clients and also to identify new ones.

In the process evaluation, the evaluation research must tap the opinions of program staff and clients. They are the primary sources for what happened during program implementation. The report clearly identifies the issues raised by clients and outreach workers by providing the results of survey data. Since the clients had long and serious arrest records, it was difficult to prepare them for and gain entry to the world of legitimate work. Overcoming this problem and gaining the trust of clients (particularly that the program was not a part of the police department) was a paramount challenge.

It is also important to describe the nature of the client population and whether their attributes mesh with the factors identified in the original design of the program as crucial to the target population. The research results revealed that the clients fit the high-risk factors listed in the original design for the target population of the program. The program evaluators also surveyed the clients and obtained data from the records maintained at the site level. The survey also tapped the client's opinions about the program's services and operations. Data analysis and graphic presentations indicate that the clients were satisfied with how the program identified and dealt with their problems. However, though the clients sought help to improve their educational and job status, these services did not always result in a successful placement. Movement out of gang involvement was documented—down to 70% from the initial 90–95% level for program clients. Client interview data supplemented data provided by the survey. Clients reported that involvement in drug treatment and anger management classes and enrollment in GED completion programs were beneficial. Involvement with the outreach workers and the program site itself helped to provide safe havens from gang involvement.

The program evaluator must identify and frankly present management issues that arose during program implementation. Often, these problems were unanticipated. Therefore, they can be of particular interest to others interested in adopting a similar approach. In Chicago, there was some reported friction between the host organization and their need to coordinate service delivery and the resulting reporting requirements required of outreach workers. Overall, the performance of the outreach workers was classified as exceptional, but turnover was a particularly vexing problem. The job was taxed by high risks, low wages, and low benefits. This precarious situation led most outreach workers to seek and maintain other employment that impacted their ability to provide program services. Other problems, such as drug use, returning to illegal work practices, inability to do the job, and personality conflicts, contributed to the turnover problem. The evaluators recommended that compensation be adjusted to deal with these problems. Therefore, while the life experience of the outreach workers gave them credibility with the program clients, they also presented an obstacle that they would have to address continually. In a way, they required some of the same treatment that their clients did because they continued to share the same problems.

The program evaluator must consider how implementation issues affect service delivery. As could be predicted, the CeaseFire turnover problem affected relationships with clients because it affected their stability. Outreach workers were simultaneously considered by clients as peers and mentors. Such personal relationships are difficult to establish and maintain. The outreach workers also faced the difficulty of maintaining the safety of their clients.

Another key factor in assessing service delivery is the observation and description of how it was delivered by program staff. Detailed analysis here can reveal how the theory behind the program was put into action. The report should explain how these observations were carried out and recorded. In the CeaseFire report, Chapter 5 describes how "violence interrupters" intervened and prevented the incidence and spread of gang-related violence. Free from client caseloads, the violence interrupters were expected to mediate conflicts before they escalated into shootings. The program evaluators collected information from personal interviews and a systematic survey of the violence interrupters during weekly meetings or by providing a survey to be mailed in later. The researchers noted that the violence interrupters disliked filling out these surveys because they had difficulty specifying how they operated in response to specific questions—they offered only vague descriptions of the conflicts and how they settled them. They were also concerned about maintaining confidentiality and protecting their clients from police sanctions. They also noted that they had difficulty maintaining a nonviolent approach to resolving conflicts themselves. The report addresses issues that were related to the conflict resolution process including race, gender, age, geography, and the influence of relatives. This is an example of how program evaluators can consider the effect of specific variables on service delivery.

Also presented here is a description of how the violence interruption meetings were held and conducted. Such information helps readers determine how persons participated in the program, their individual characteristics, who participated in meetings, and how they conducted themselves. In short, it provides an analysis of how the program brought the program theory to life.

The more detailed and specific the nature of service delivery provided, the better the information provided to the reader. In Chicago, the violence interrupters faced a number of issues on a regular basis. They were continually on the street, waiting for incidences to develop that would require intervention—in other words, "hanging out." As a result, they were constantly confronted with dangerous situations that threatened their personal safety. The program evaluators noted that this was a significant program problem because CeaseFire did not protect them by providing health benefits. Their role was often misperceived by the clients who thought they were linked to the police and by the police who wondered if they were committing illegal acts. Their mediation skills focused on working with street networks to stop shootings and used personal connections to mediate conflicts. However, not all conflicts could be mediated, especially those unpredictable incidents that were rooted in gang turf conflicts, retaliation, and "respect." In this fashion, the program evaluators provided interpretations of how the violence interrupters viewed their job and conducted their business—often in idiosyncratic ways.

Another crucial aspect of the CeaseFire model was to provide support through community organizations. Here, Chapter 6 documents how networks of collaborating organizations grew and developed in the program sites. The organizations that participated were clergy, service agencies (e.g., schools providing GED programs), local businesses, police, and political leaders. Here again, program evaluators conducted personal interviews with members of these groups, attended meetings, and examined meeting records to determine how they worked within the program. The frequency of service provision and the organizations involved were recorded and presented graphically. Case studies of organizations were provided that explicated how they conducted their program business by sharing information with others and involvement in hiring of clients. The case study of clergy involvement noted that they were especially effective in providing a safe haven from violence.

In sum, the process evaluation describes the context of the program in action. It provides information on what actually took place in service delivery, what the service actually was, who delivered it, how they delivered it, and the strengths and weaknesses of their approaches. Staffing the program is presented as well as the opinions of program participants. Thus, the program and its services are no longer abstract ideas. The process evaluation gives them concrete form and life.

Presenting the Impact Evaluation

The results of the impact evaluation are the meat of the evaluation—where results are quantified and assessed in terms of how goals were met. Conclusions are reached and supporting data are presented. The findings are presented in detail in the body of the report and also in the program summary. The summary is a crucial aspect of the report because it is the first section consulted by readers.

In the CeaseFire report, Chapter 7 is the impact evaluation and describes the effect of CeaseFire on shootings and killings in the target areas. Naturally, this chapter is a more detailed presentation than that contained in the summary. This chapter discusses the methodology and statistical analysis in some detail. The summary focuses on a presentation of the results alone in a nontechnical fashion but with conclusions firmly stated. Chapter 8 of the report presents a summary of the program evaluation findings.

The impact analysis focused on seven sites served by the program that had been in operation for a sufficient amount of time to permit statistical analysis (ARIMA time-series analysis—see Chapter 6 of this book). Comparison group areas were constructed by matching these areas with the seven targeted sites on several variables, including home ownership, racial composition, family organization, and poverty. The outcome variables considered the impact of the program on shootings and killings, plus a consideration of how the program affected hot-spot crime areas, which is one of the reasons why areas were originally selected as program sites. Also examined were the effects of the program on gang networks. In Chapter 7 of the report, these analyses were presented in detail with summary tables and geographic maps for each area. In addition to the research findings, the limitations of the study are also presented and accounted for in this report chapter.

In terms of impact on violence, CeaseFire was effective in reducing shootings (decline ranged from − 16% to − 27%), the "cooling" of hot spots (violence declining from − 15% to − 40%), and gang homicide reduced in six of the seven areas served by the program. The key limitation on these findings is that all of Chicago had experienced a dramatic decline in violent crime since 1992.

A singular feature of the summary chapter in the CeaseFire report is that the entire report and all of the chapters, not just the outcome analysis, is provided. Such a design allows readers to move to the final chapter and consult the chapters only when they have a specific question about the findings.

In sum, the CeaseFire report examined in this chapter provides an excellent example of how criminal justice evaluation should be presented. It is informative, well designed, and written with detailed analyses and careful consideration of the limitations of the research.

Factors Influencing the Use of Program Evaluation Results

Evaluation research findings are not automatically adopted by the criminal justice system. For example, Innes & Everett (2008) review the problems that hinder the use of research to guide criminal justice operations. One of their key arguments is the failure of researchers and practitioners to clearly communicate with one another. The main problem here is a difference in perspective. Researchers tend to focus on explanations of social science methodology and analysis to determine "what works" in criminal justice, while practitioners, however eager to receive and utilize such information, are looking for language that will tell them how to do it (Innes & Everett, 2008, p. 50). Researchers value objectivity and remaining "value-free," while practitioners are seeking pragmatic solutions to crime problems. As a result, they call for a more productive partnership collaboration between the two groups with a division of labor to bridge the gap between the generation of knowledge and the business of practice: "The solution lies in the acceptance by both the research and practitioner communities of the hard work involved in sharing the control and responsibility of the entire process of building new knowledge in the service of the public good" (Innes & Everett, 2008, p. 56).

Echoing these concerns, Synder (2011) calls for a socially responsible criminology that attempts to get both data and information into the hands of policy makers and administrators. Criminologists must recognize that policy makers cannot wait for "perfect" information—they must often go with what they have. Information from program and policy evaluations can fill this void to the satisfaction of all. Again, Synder stresses the necessity to present research results in a usable and easily understandable format when written and when presented in a face-to-face meeting.

One of the crucial factors in the utilization of evaluation results is to first identify the stakeholders in the process. One definition of stakeholders is "individuals, groups, or organizations that can affect or are affected by an evaluation process and/or its findings" (Bryson, Patton & Bowman, 2011, p. 1). Stakeholders are significant to the evaluation process because they can contribute to the validity of the research design, data collected, and interpretation of the findings of the final report. Therefore, the identification of such stakeholders is key to the success of the evaluation itself. Bryson & colleagues (2011, p. 7) offer a method to identify key stakeholders ("primary intended users") according to their contribution to the conduct and ultimate use of the evaluation results.

A review of the research on the utilization of evaluation research results (Leviton & Hughes, 1981) determined that there were five factors that influenced this process:

1. The relevance of the evaluation to the needs of potential users. The research should contain information about implementation and the effectiveness of program elements.
2. The extent of communication between potential users and producers of evaluations.
3. The translations of evaluations into their implications for policies and programs. This information must be clearly presented and answer specific questions about the probable effect of a program or policy.
4. The credibility or trust placed in evaluations. Here, use of an unassailable methodology is important.
5. Commitment or advocacy by individual users.

Addressing these factors will help the evaluation researcher produce a credible report and increase the probability that decision makers will consult and utilize the research results.

With regard to program evaluation, O'Sullivan (2012, p. 518) promotes "collaborative evaluation," which assumes that active, ongoing engagement between evaluators and program staff will result in stronger evaluation designs, enhanced data collection and analysis, and results that stakeholders understand and use. It promotes cooperation and participation throughout the program evaluation process, recognizing and valuing the experience and expertise of all groups toward the use of a research design that is as rigorous as possible under the circumstances. It recognizes that stakeholders can serve as "clients, partners, evaluation assistants and data sources" (O'Sullivan, 2012, p. 520). Their engagement will improve the validity and accuracy of the evaluation process.

This process requires the evaluation researcher to reach conclusions based on the research evidence and state them clearly. Tables 9.1 and 9.2 present a summary of how to examine and reach conclusions from the process and impact evaluations. Using an example from problem-oriented policing, Clarke & Eck (2005, p. 104) provide diagrams that summarize this process. In Table 9.1, the questions to be answered by the process evaluation are:

1. Was the program put into place as planned?
2. How did it change during implementation?

The process implementation focuses on inputs (personnel, equipment, expenditures, and other resources) and results (arrests, people trained, barriers installed, or other tasks accomplished). The focus of the impact evaluation is on outcomes (crimes reduced, fear abated, accidents reduced, and other reductions in problems).

Table 9.1 Focus of Process and Impact Evaluations

Process Evaluation Focus

Inputs	Results
Personnel	Arrests
Equipment	People trained
Expenditures	Barriers installed
Other resources	Other tasks accomplished

Impact Evaluation Focus

Outcomes

Crimes reduced
Fear abated
Accidents reduced
Other reductions in problems

Source: Clarke & Eck (2005), p. 104.

Table 9.2 Interpreting Results of Process and Impact Evaluations

	Process Evaluation Results	Response Implemented as Planned	Response Not Implemented as Planned
Impact Evaluation Results	Problem declined and no other likely cause	A. Evidence that the response caused the decline.	C. Suggests that the response was accidentally effective or that other factors may have caused the decline.
	Problem did not decline	B. Evidence that the response was ineffective.	D. Little is learned.

Source: Clarke & Eck (2005), p. 104.

Table 9.2 summarizes the possible conclusions reached on the basis of the process and impact evaluation findings. In cell A, the process evaluation results determined that the response was implemented as planned and the impact evaluation found that the problem declined and there was no other likely cause (other than the response). Therefore, the conclusion is that the research produced evidence that the response caused the decline.

In cell B, the process evaluation results determined that the response was implemented as planned and the impact evaluation found that the problem did not decline. Therefore, the conclusion is that the evaluation results found evidence that the response was ineffective.

In cell C, the process evaluation results determined that the response was not implemented as planned and the impact evaluation found that the problem declined and there was no other likely cause (other than the response). The conclusion is that the response was accidentally effective or that other factors may have caused the decline.

Finally, in cell D, the process evaluation results determined that the response was not implemented as planned and the impact evaluation found that the problem did not decline. Therefore, little is learned from the research results. It could also be surmised that the program failed to accomplish its goals.

Summary

As noted in this chapter, the program evaluator must pay careful attention to the construction and presentation of the final report. It is the result of a long process of hard work, and it is the final and most important product of the evaluation research process. How it is written and presented will determine whether the findings are used by program administrators, decision makers, and other concerned persons. Special attention must be given to these audiences, especially program stakeholders. To a large extent, their participation made the research possible and their interest in the research results is often personal. The CeaseFire report is an excellent example of how criminal justice evaluation research should be presented and written.

Discussion Questions

1. What are the parts of an evaluation research report and why are they important?
2. How should they be presented?

3. What are the factors influencing the use of an evaluation research report by program administrators and decision makers?
4. Apply Clarke and Eck's framework (Tables 9.1 and 9.2) to Operation CeaseFire. What are your conclusions?

References

Bryson, J. M., Patton, M. Q., & Bowman, R. A. (2011). Working with evaluation stakeholders: A rationale, step-wise approach and toolkit. *Evaluation and Program Planning, 34*, 1-12.

Clarke, R. V., & Eck, J. E. (2005). *Crime analysis for problem solvers in 60 small steps.* Washington, DC: U.S. Department of Justice, Office of Community-Oriented Policing Services.

Innes, C. A., & Everett, R. S. (2008). Factors and conditions influencing the use of research in the criminal justice system. *Western Criminology Review, 9*(1), 49-58.

Leviton, L. C., & Hughes, E. F. (1981). Research on the utilization of evaluations: A review and synthesis. *Evaluation Research, 5*(4), 525-548.

Lipton, D. S. (1992). How to maximize utilization of evaluation research by policymakers. *Annals of the American Academy of Political and Social Science, 521*, 175-188.

O'Sullivan, R. G. (2012). Collaborative evaluation within a framework of stakeholder-oriented evaluation approaches. *Evaluation and Program Planning, 35*, 518-522.

Skogan, W. G., Hartnett, S. M., Bump, N., & Dubois, J. (2008). *Evaluation of CeaseFire Chicago.* Chicago: Northwestern University. Available online at < *www.ncjrs.gov/pdffiles1/nij/grants/227181.pdf* >.

Synder, H. N. (2011). Socially responsible criminology: Quality relevant research with targeted, effective dissemination. *Criminology and Public Policy, 10*(2), 207-215.

Weiss, C. (1998). *Evaluation research: Methods for assessing program effectiveness.* Englewood Cliffs, NJ: Prentice-Hall.

10

LOOKING AHEAD: A CALL TO ACTION IN EVALUATION RESEARCH

Keywords

crime displacement
diffusion of benefits
public value

CHAPTER OUTLINE
Introduction   142
Point 1: Use the Best Possible Research Design   142
Point 2: Evaluators must get Involved in the Very Beginning of the Program   142
Point 3: Evaluators must Include Some Measure of Cost in their Analyses   143
Point 4: Evaluation Leads to the Development of Evidence-Based Practice   144
Point 5: Get out into the Field   144
Point 6: Prepare to Partner with Practitioners   145
Conclusion   146
Discussion Questions   146
References   147

In this new wave of collaborations, the academic researcher is a partner who works with the group toward an end. The academic is not a critic who focuses on past mistakes and ineffective practices or a miracle worker who will solve crime problems by developing magic bullets.

—Anthony A. Braga & Marianne Hinkle (2010, p. 114)

Introduction

Throughout this text, we have emphasized a number of key points and issues relating to the conduct of evaluation research. In this chapter, we reaffirm and reinforce these principles by repeating them and documenting how criminologists in general have written about them.

Point 1: Use the Best Possible Research Design

Research must use the best possible designs that will document comparisons between the program outcomes and what would have resulted if nothing was done. The quality of the research design can help dispel long held myths and misconceptions about criminal justice operations and tactics. For a number of years, criminologists held the view that the police truly could do nothing about crime because the social causes that contributed to it were far beyond their scope and reach. However, experiments have documented the effectiveness of hot-spot policing (concentrating efforts on high-crime locations) for public safety. Not only does the "focused police resources on crime hot spots provide the strongest collective evidence of police effectiveness," it also debunks the notion of crime displacement (i.e., that crime will simply move to other areas rather than being truly impacted) by demonstrating a "diffusion of benefits"—that crime control spreads to areas beyond the target location (Nagin & Weisburd, 2013, p. 655).

Here we must repeat two key methodological issues. First, it is necessary that all evaluations have either a control or comparison group or a baseline measure of what the crime rate was before the program was implemented (Weatherburn, 2009, p. 2). Second, it is important to combine quantitative and qualitative methods to improve the understanding of the evaluation findings (Leeuw, 2005, p. 254).

Point 2: Evaluators must get Involved in the Very Beginning of the Program

Evaluation researchers must take a hands-on approach to test theories and develop programs that are based on sound research findings. They must be involved at the very beginning of programs and their development to ensure that the program is properly implemented and that data are collected that will validly measure both the process and impact (outcome) evaluation. For example, Sherman (2006, p. 395) urges criminologists to become actively involved in the "design, development and implementation of anti-crime programs." He emphasizes this point by documenting the fact that "anti-crime programs are more likely to be found effective if the same experimental social scientists contributed to the program development and the program evaluation" (Sherman, 2006, p. 399). Researchers must become involved in the program early in its development so that they can follow the policy and program processes as they evolve and identify the opportunities for evaluation, such as the opportunity to conduct a natural experiment, implement an experimental design, or opt for a quasi-experimental design (Nagin & Weisburd, 2013, p. 671).

Point 3: Evaluators must Include Some Measure of Cost in their Analyses

Cost analysis must be included in these efforts. Cost is the one variable that everyone understands. Plus, it demonstrates whether the program will make the criminal justice system more cost efficient and thus make public dollars available for other governmental services (e.g., housing, transportation, education, health services).

Including cost analysis in meta-analyses, Drake, Aos & Miller (2009) provided research evidence to help decision makers in Washington state determine what programs to adopt in an attempt to improve public safety and reduce the prison population. Their review determined that cognitive-based programs for offenders while in prison or on parole reduced recidivism by 6.9% (Drake et al., 2009, p. 191). They determined that the cognitive-behavioral programs had the potential to generate a savings of $15,361 per person (Drake et al., 2009, p. 193). Specially designed family-based therapies for juveniles reduced their recidivism rates by over 18% for "functional family therapy, "and over 38% percent for "nurse–family partnerships" (Drake et al., 2009, p. 192). These programs could result in a savings of over $49,000 for the functional family therapy program and over $20,000 for the nurse–family partnership. Analysis of this information also led to the conclusion that, if Washington state adopted a portfolio of "moderate to aggressive" evidence-based options, crime could be reduced and a savings of about $2 billion in prison construction could be achieved (Aos et al., 2006, p. 275). By combining recidivism and program costs, this research gives decision makers a more complete picture of the potential effectiveness of programs.

Citing a more subtle notion of cost, Moore (2002, p. 38) stresses the need to assess the "public value" of a program or policy in the evaluation research process. What is the value of the effect of a program? This question requires an assessment of not only if the program worked better than others in achieving the same (or better) result, but also whether the effectiveness of the policy was sufficient enough to justify the resources required to produce the results. In terms of dollars, the issue is whether tax dollars might be better spent on some other governmental initative or problem. Specifically, Moore (2002) gives the example of whether a police program that reduces crime is worth it in terms of its cost to individual liberty. These questions require the consideration of issues other than financial costs and savings.

Point 4: Evaluation Leads to the Development of Evidence-Based Practice

Program evaluation is one of the best ways to inform evidence-based practice. Evidence-based practice is the way of the future across program evaluation. Well-designed and executed program evaluations can inform public policy by demonstrating whether criminal justice programs are effective at all levels. Meta-analyses will further enhance this process by compiling and ascertaining the impact of a particular policy or program on an across the board scale by extending the analysis beyond the findings of one isolated program.

For example, Landenberger & Lipsey (2005) conducted a meta-analysis of 58 experimental and quasi-experimental studies of cognitive-behavioral programs (CBTs) for offenders. The programs under review featured CBT therapies such as anger control and interpersonal problem solving. Overall, offenders treated in CBTs registered a 25% lower recidivism rate than untreated offenders (Landenberger & Lipsey, 2005, p. 470). In addition, the effect sizes for the CBT therapies were influenced by the risk level of the offender (high-risk offenders did better), how well the treatment was implemented (programs with low dropout rates did better), and stronger effects were noted for anger control and problem solving than those for victim impact and behavior modification components (Landenberger & Lipsey, 2005, p. 470). These findings underscore the need for evaluation researchers to specify the nature of the treatment and the implementation and operations of the program (the process evaluation). It is necessary to include measures of program integrity and quality in evaluation research (Latessa, 2004, p. 552). This research provides specific information about the CBTs that the research determined to be most effective.

Point 5: Get out into the Field

Program evaluation contributes to a researcher's development by getting him or her out to the front lines where the action is to see firsthand what is going on in terms of crime, delinquency, drug abuse, or violence. By its very nature, evaluation research requires that the researcher must leave the safety of academe and get his or her hands "dirty." It is the research equivalent of "management by walking around" (MBWA). There is no substitute for this direct experience. In addition, it gives the researcher the opportunity to test theories directly in the field and generate primary data. Thus, it enriches the researcher's understanding of how criminal justice agencies operate and the real-world obstacles that practitioners routinely encounter. In addition, evaluation research extends the understanding of what the clients of criminal justice agencies face, both victims and offenders.

Evaluation researchers must also take extraordinary steps to communicate the results of their studies to practitioners. The research results must be presented in a clear fashion to those outlets that practitioners routinely consume—their publications and making presentations at their conferences and training sessions. Latessa (2004, p. 552) urges researchers to "leave the office" and "be willing to attend and present at nonacademic conferences, conduct workshops for local professionals, and in general be willing to lend our expertise and knowledge when asked to do so."

Point 6: Prepare to Partner with Practitioners

As we have discussed in the text, practitioners view the evaluation research process differently than academics. Wilson (2006) stresses the need to continue to evaluate criminal justice programs and makes several comparisons to pharmaceutical research. Resistance to criminal justice program evaluation may arise from the fact that its policy recommendations may require reorganization of institutions, rewarding some individuals while disadvantaging others, and changes in how agencies are funded. Although the criminal justice system is faced with declining financial resources, making a program or policy available may save monies but still involve considerable political risk if the initiative fails.

Practitioners are invested in tactics. They need information to guide policy and programs. While academics offer research expertise, practitioners know the front-line operations of their agency and have direct experience with the problems that they face. They provide access to data and real-world sites that academics may have trouble obtaining on their own. They also know what their program or policy is designed to do and the academics can put this knowledge into research hypotheses for analysis. It is important for academics to understand their place in this process and build trust with practitioners (Braga & Hinkle, 2010).

Skogan (2010) reminds us that practitioners require timeliness and utility from the evaluation research process. These needs may also lead to conflict because the research process requires time to properly construct the research design, accurately collect data (both quantitative and qualitative), analyze the data, and write the report and findings in understandable terms (Skogan, 2010, pp. 128–130). Again, academics must make this information availble to practitioners by first conducting briefing sessions and then presenting and publishing findings in practitioner publications and at their conferences and workshops.

In sum, evaluation research gives academics an opportunity to have an impact on criminal justice by extending their knowledge-building role to their communities. In this fashion, research findings can become truly relevant.

Conclusion

Evaluation research offers hope for the future—a future that will lead to effective crime prevention and treatment. Leeuw (2005, pp. 237–238) offers several reasons why evaluation research has grown and become important. First, it is tied to the need for governmental operations to be transparent and accountable. Second, evaluation stimulates organizational learning by showing administrators how things can be improved. Third, it can show what programs and policies are most effective. Finally, it promotes the development of evidence-based practice and thus generates knowledge about programs and their effectiveness.

It is our hope that the materials presented and issues discussed in this book will lead to improved evaluation methods in criminal justice research. Information is needed to guide policy and ensure that operations are effective.

Discussion Questions

1. Why is evidence-based practice important?
2. How can evaluation research inform evidence-based practice?
3. Why is it important to get out into the field?
4. Why is cost analysis an important part of program evaluation?
5. Why is it important to reach practitioners with evaluation research findings?

References

Aos, S., Miller, M., & Drake, E. (2006). Evidence-based policy options to reduce future prison construction, criminal justice costs, and crime rates. *Federal Sentencing Reporter, 19*(4), 275-290.

Braga, A. A., & Hinkle, M. (2010). The participation of academics in the criminal justice working group process. In J. Klofas, N. K. Hipple, & E. McGarrell (Eds.), *The new criminal justice: American communities and the changing world of crime control* (pp. 114-120). New York: Routledge.

Drake, E. K., Aos, S., & Miller, M. G. (2009). Evidence-based public policy options to reduce crime and criminal justice costs: Implications in Washington State. *Victims and Offenders, 4*, 170-196.

Landenberger, N. A., & Lipsey, M. A. (2005). The postive effects of cognitive-behavioral programs for offenders: A meta-analysis of factors associated with effective treatment. *Journal of Experimental Criminology, 1*, 451-476.

Latessa, E. J. (2004). The challenge of change: Correctional programs and evidence-based practices. *Criminology and Public Policy, 3*(4), 547-560.

Leeuw, F. (2005). Trends and developments in program evaluation in general and criminal justice programs in particular. *European Journal on Criminal Policy and Research, 11*, 233-258.

Moore, M. H. (2002). The limits of social science in guiding policy. *Criminology and Public Policy, 2*(1), 33-42.

Nagin, D. S., & Weisburd, D. (2013). Evidence and public policy: The example of evaluation research in policing. *Criminology and Public Policy, 12*(4), 651-679.

Sherman, L. W. (2006). "To Develop and Test": The inventive difference between evaluation and experimentation. *Journal of Experimental Criminology, 2*, 393-406.

Skogan, W. (2010). The challenge of timeliness and utility in research and evaluation. In J. Klofas, N. K. Hipple, & E. McGarrell (Eds.), *The new criminal justice: American communities and the changing world of crime control* (pp. 128-137). New York: Routledge.

Weatherburn, D. (2009). *Policy and program evaluation: Recommendations for criminal justice policy analysts and advisors*. Sydney, Australia: NSW Bureau of Crime Statistics and Research.

Wilson, J. Q. (2006). The need for evaluation research. *Journal of Experimental Criminology, 2*, 321-328.

GLOSSARY

Before-and-after design This design features the comparison between the performance of the same group before (pre-test) and after (post-test) exposure to the experimental treatment (X). However, it is a weak type of design because the researcher will be unable to be certain that the experimental treatment (X) is responsible for the difference (if one exists) before and after the measurement is taken. The only comparison made is within the experimental group.

Campbell Collaboration (Crime and Justice Group) This organization sponsors and encourages the development of rigorous and valid evaluation reports that can contribute to the policy-making process. The Crime and Justice Group aims to prepare and maintain systematic reviews of crime programs and policies and make them electronically accessible through its website (http://www.campbellcollaboration.org/crime_and_justice/index.php) to all concerned parties.

Classic experimental design This design features a crucial comparison in outcome results between the treatment (receives the services of the program) and control (untreated) groups. The key feature is that the groups are selected *at random* from a pool of candidates from the target population that the program is designed to serve. Basically, the classic experimental design measures the impact of a program by applying it to the treatment group, withholding it from the control group, and then measuring what happened as a result of the experiment.

Community forums These forums differ in how the individuals are selected to participate. In focus groups, demographics are the thrust behind the decision to include an individual. Community forums are a self-selected group. When programs or policies on a large scale are up for consideration, agencies—government or private—may announce the date and time of a community meeting to consider some planning issue.

Comparison group In place of a control group, quasi-experimental research features the use of a comparison (untreated) group that is constructed by some method other than random assignment.

Conceptualization The process of specifying the meaning of the terms in the evaluation.

Construct validity The adequacy of the operational definition of program outcomes and other measurements in the program evaluation that track the program interventions. Threats to construct validity include whether the program succeeded in making intended changes in outcome (treatment fidelity or failure in program implementation), the validity and reliability of program outcome measures, ascertaining the level of crime displacement or the diffusion of program benefits, and contamination of the program treatment (control group exposure to the treatment).

Control group The control group is designed to ensure the comparison in program outcomes with the experimental group. Random assignment guarantees that the two groups are equal and alike in every aspect except for their exposure to the program.

Cost-benefit analysis The calculation of costs versus the benefits of a program.

Cost-effectiveness analysis Seeks to identify and place dollar value on the cost of the program.

Crime displacement The assumption that police crackdowns (e.g., hot-spot policing) will simply move crime to adjacent or other areas of a city.

Descriptive validity The adequacy of presentation of key evaluation features in the research report. Including previously mentioned indicators, evaluations should include such factors as the description of the treatment received, the follow-up period after the program intervention, and conflict-of-interest issues (Who funded the intervention? How independent were the researchers?).

Diffusion of benefits A research finding from hot-spot policing studies that found crime control benefits, not crime displacement, extended to the areas adjacent to the police operation.

Evaluability assessment approach An evaluability assessment refers to a method of identifying and describing the program theory by outlining its components and deciphering which of these components is measurable.

Experimental group Within the classic experiment, the purpose of random assignment is to guarantee that the two groups are equal and alike in every aspect except for their exposure to the program. That is the one and only difference between the groups that the classic experiment wishes to preserve and ultimately examine. The experimental group gets the program and the control group does not. Therefore, any difference in outcomes should be logically attributable to the exposure to the program and not to other factors beyond the control of the evaluator. If there is a treatment effect, it should be present in the performance of the experimental group and not the control group.

External validity The generalizability of program findings to other settings. Of course, this is the purpose of systematic reviews of evaluations via the quality of their research design. The effect size of the program intervention is also a key indicator of value.

Focus group A specialized method of interviewing where the researcher interviews a group of people at one time. A focus group is a group discussion usually consisting of 6–12 individuals. The discussion is used to obtain in-depth information from participants regarding attitudes, beliefs, behaviors, and opinions.

Host organization The home of a program with more than one location or partner.

Hot spots Areas of a city that are proven to be consistent sites of violence.

Impact theory Provides instances about the change process and the change in the conditions.

Interviewing A structured conversation with an individual. Here, the evaluator provides a format for the discussion by determining the questions to be asked, ordering them in a particular way, and determining the time and place of the interview. The aim is to ensure the accuracy of the information gathered during the interview. The assumption is that an interview will capture information that cannot be observed by the evaluator and tap into the subject's thoughts about the program, its operations, and its implementation.

Internal validity Whether the program intervention really did cause a change in program outcomes. Of course, the experimental design with the use of random assignment to experimental and control groups is the best mechanism to ensure internal validity.

Key informants Individuals who know the criminal justice system or their part of the criminal justice system and may know what needs are going unmet.

Logic model Often presented in the form of a diagram, the logic model specifies the conceptual framework of an evaluation by establishing the variables to be measured and the expected relationships among them. It provides an explanation of how the program is expected to work and how the program goals, processes, resources, and outcomes will provide the direction for the program. Thus, they provide a clear "roadmap" of what is planned and expected results—a review of the strength of the connection between activities and outcomes.

"Maryland Report" This report is an example of a systematic review of existing research on criminal justice programs and identifies those determined to be most effective. To make these classifications, they developed the Maryland scale of scientific methods:
- The control of other variables that might have been the true causes of any connection between the program and crime.
- Measurement error from such matters as loss of subjects over time or low interview response rates.
- Statistical power to detect the magnitude of program effects.

Mean The arithmetic average of a distribution of numbers.

Median The middle most number of a distribution of numbers.

Meta-analysis The most sophisticated form of systematic review. Specifically, it calculates an effect size across studies of a particular crime problem or policy that reveals the strength of the impact of the particular treatment on the dependent variable to make a comparative determination of effectiveness.

Mode The most commonly occurring number of a distribution of numbers.

Need An assessment of need is important because it improves the quality of program planning. Planners or evaluators are not able to develop a comprehensive set of program objectives when the needs of the program are not explicitly known. This means that the program may operate inefficiently or ineffectively, which is not a good way to use scarce resources. Needs assessments may not always provide the most comprehensive information. Many needs assessments do not fully consider the need of the intended individuals. This is to say that program planners and evaluators may create a program that does not meet the desired needs. Further, many programs do not seem to take the context of the program into account. Many programs do not consider that a community, a correctional institution, or law enforcement may not have the capacity to handle the program. With all of this information in mind, planning a program may begin.

Observer as participant A role assumed by the evaluator where the research subjects (program administrators, staff, and clients) know evaluator's role, identity, and purpose. The observations of the evaluator are overt and announced. Program administrators, staff, and participants know that the evaluator is present and observations are being made. The evaluator is free to ask questions and directly observe program activities at any site and location. There is no need for the evaluation research to assume any other role or to hide the attempts at direct observation.

One-group time-series design An expansion of the before-and after design, the time-series design features more frequent measures taken before and after the introduction of the treatment (X) variable. The use of several tests given over a period of time gives the researcher more control over possible threats to internal validity.

Operational definition The actual statement or questions that are designed to capture information about the dimensions or indicators.

Operation CeaseFire A Chicago-based program designed to reduce gun violence by gang members.

Opportunity cost Planners have to consider the cost of the program being considered and the cost of other programs. This will allow the planner to better understand the choices between the considered program and alternative programs.

Outcome evaluation The purpose of the outcome evaluation is to evaluate the impact of the program and to determine the extent to which it achieved its goals. The research results can be used to guide the decision of policy makers on whether to maintain, expand, or terminate the program. The outcome evaluation features the use of quantitative research methods and several types of research designs.

Problem-oriented policing A method of policing that attempts to address crime problems rather than just respond to calls for service. The police use strategic thinking, planning, and operations to address the sources of crime problems, both individual and systemic.

Process evaluation The purpose of the process evaluation is to monitor the implementation of the project and provide feedback to guide program operations. The acquired information can be used to maintain and strengthen program aspects that are effective and alter those revealed to be ineffective. The process evaluation features the use of qualitative research methods—in particular, the use of observation and interviewing of both individuals and groups.

Program organizational plan Written from the perspective of program management. This plan brings together the functions and activities of the program.

Program theory Prioritizing questions, research designs, and interpreting evaluation findings. This type of theory does not have to be a formal theory, but one that is integrative.

Propensity score matching (PSM) Another method of constructing an equivalent comparison group in a quasi-experimental design. PSM is designed to reduce the selection bias that is often a problem in quasi-experimental design. The propensity score is generated via a logistic regression model that estimates the probability of group selection. Selection into the treatment group (0 = no selection; 1 = selection) is the dependent variable in the logistic regression model. Thus, PSM creates treatment and comparison groups by using the likelihood of observed characteristic in the groups (i.e., independent variables like race, gender, age, drug history, criminal offense, etc.) and balances the groups in terms of these observed characteristics.

Public value The concept that the assessment of the benefit of a program must go beyond simple measures of cost to their relationship to more abstract concepts like justice and liberty.

Quasi-experimental design This design preserves the crucial comparison in program outcomes between a treated (experimental) and untreated group of program participants. It is typically applied when the setting does not permit the use of the classic experiment. Thus, the quasi-experiment attempts to maintain some measure of experimental rigor and control over relevant variables other than the treatment by some method other than random assignment.

Rate of return The amount the benefit will return from expending the funds.

SARA The heart of the problem-oriented policing process. It consists of four steps:
- *Scanning:* Identify recurring problems and how they affect community safety.
- *Analysis:* Determine the causes of the problem.
- *Response:* Seeking out, selecting, and implementing activities to solve the problem.
- *Assessment:* Determine if the response was effective or identify new strategies.

The aim of this process is to collect data that are related to the problem, determine the validity of these data, trace causal relationships that could lead to problem identification and programs to address it, and then determine if the programs were effective in solving the problem.

Service utilization plan Vital to a theory-driven evaluation because it contains the assumptions and expectations on reaching the target population. In other words, the service utilization plan provides the proper manner to initiate and terminate the service.

S.M.A.R.T. A method designed to ensure that goals are stated in a measurable fashion. Well-defined goals should be:
- *Specific:* Goals must be clear and specific. They should represent what the program is trying to accomplish and accurately measure successful operations.
- *Measureable:* If the goal is not measurable, there is no way to gauge progress.
- *Attainable:* Again, goals must be realistic. Some effort and stretching is always in order, but goals should neither be too high or too low that they become meaningless.
- *Relevant:* The goals should represent and mirror the program's vision and mission.
- *Time-bound:* Goals must have starting and end points, and the duration of the measurement should be stated clearly.

Self-drop group A comparison group that is often used in correctional program evaluations, the self-drop group typically consists of subjects who were not officially denied access to the program although they met the criteria for program eligibility. They did not participate for nonprejudicial reasons of their own, such as they had been paroled earlier than expected, they entered other programs while waiting and did not want to drop them, or they changed their minds while waiting.

Social indicators Show changes in conditions that provide some insight that a problem or need exists. Tracking official records of crime, delinquency, unemployment of parolees, recidivism, or school dropout rates may provide some indication of the types of problems that could influence criminal justice. Increases in these types of social indicators suggest a need for a program, but when these problems are addressed properly through carefully thought-out planning and programming, they will be lower.

Statistical conclusion validity Concerned with whether the program intervention and the program outcomes are related. The main threats to it are insufficient statistical power (the probability of rejecting the null hypothesis when it is false) and the use of statistical techniques that are inappropriate when the data violate the assumptions behind the statistical test.

Standard deviation The square root of the variance. This becomes the single number that is representative of the deviations from the mean found in that data distribution. The standard deviation is important for data that are at least ordinal. The importance of the standard deviation for the evaluator is that it provides information on the type of deviation from the mean. With a normal distribution, two-thirds of the distribution should be within one standard deviation of the mean.

Systematic review These reviews feature use of rigorous methods to locate, appraise, and synthesize findings from criminal justice program evaluation studies. Typically, they give their criteria for including studies, conduct an extensive search to find them, code their key features (especially their methodology), and provide conclusions of their assessment.

Threats to external validity To assess the external validity of a design, the program evaluator must also be concerned about:
- *Interaction effects of selection bias:* In terms of the drug court example, clients of the program may have different types of drug problems, levels of addiction, and types of crimes committed, not to mention differences in intelligence or socioeconomic status. Such differences could affect the confidence of the program evaluator that the drug court program will achieve the same results in another location.
- *Reactive effect of pre-testing:* A pre-test can increase the sensitivity of the research subjects. Again, if the drug court clients were given a drug test as a part of the pre-testing procedure for the drug court evaluation, they may be more or less aware of their potential to return to drug abuse. Therefore, the experimental group may no longer be comparable to those in need of the drug court program elsewhere.
- *Reactive effect of experimental procedures:* The experiment is a treatment in and of itself, if the subjects become aware of the fact that they are being studied. Drug court clients may have altered their drug use because they were aware that they were part of the program evaluation. Therefore, they are no longer representative of the population that drug courts are attempting to reach.
- *Multiple treatment inference:* If the drug court treatment has several aspects (e.g., drug counseling and drug testing), how does the evaluator know which of these treatment features were responsible for the results of the experiment?

The evaluator must be attentive to these threats to the generalizability of not only the research findings but also with respect to other settings, independent (treatment) variables, and outcome measures. The question is whether the findings of the outcome evaluation the evaluator has conducted are applicable to other locations.

Threats to internal validity Specifically, there are several types of internal (to the conduct of the experiment) validity problems:
- *History:* This occurs when the research subjects experience an event in addition to the treatment that may affect their performance regarding the dependent variable.
- *Maturation:* The subjects may also change via biological or psychological processes rather than exposure to the program (treatment). For example, the experimental group may perform better or worse than the control group because they grew older, were fatigued, or were less interested in the program than they were when it began. Such changes would necessarily confound conclusions concerning the effectiveness of the program.
- *Testing:* Depending on the nature of the pre-test, it may be another treatment in itself. In the drug court example, this could be an issue if the pre-test was a drug test. Any difference in post-test drug testing results could thus be due to the initial drug test (and its outcome) and not due to the treatment portion of the drug court. In other words, if a person was positive on the first test, he or she would have an incentive to do better regardless of the effect of the treatment program.
- *Instrumentation:* Changing the instrument (or measurements) used between the pre-test and the post-test will also confound the issue of program effectiveness. Any outcome could be affected by these changes in addition to exposure to the treatment.
- *Statistical regression to the mean:* This is an issue when the target population represents an extreme group, like career criminals or repeat DWI offenders. Since the group is extreme in terms of its problem, they will get "better" just because it is unlikely that they can get any "worse." Therefore, some improvement in performance could be due to this source and program effectiveness.

- *Selection bias:* If any factors other than random assignment played a role in the assignment of individuals to the experimental and control groups, selection bias is in play. For example, if individuals were referred to the drug court program because they were more amenable to treatment (i.e., were ready to change) rather than random assignment, the program could achieve good results due to this factor rather than any effort by program operatives. This is also known as *creaming*—selecting superior applicants to make the program look good.
- *Experimental mortality:* If individuals drop out of the experiment at high rates after it is underway, these losses could affect the results of the evaluation. For example, if drug court participants quit the program when they failed to pass a drug test, the experimental group may generate a lower recidivism rate on the post-test, not because of the drug court treatment but because the participants who did not abstain from drug abuse left the program, leaving those individuals who did succeed in the treatment group.
- *Masking:* The experimental treatment could have opposite or different effects on different kinds of subjects. For example, the drug court clients in the experimental group could have problems with different types of drugs (e.g., cocaine vs. marijuana or heroin vs. methamphetamine). Therefore, the drug court treatment may be more or less effective with its clients because of the source of their drug addiction.
- *Contamination of data:* This occurs when the program evaluator loses control of the experiment and both the experimental and control groups are exposed to the treatment. For example, if the control group in the drug court experiment were somehow enlisted in some aspect of the program, the result would be that the evaluation now contained one larger experimental group and no control group.
- *Erosion of the treatment effect:* This has to do with the gradual or abrupt disappearance of a successful performance of the experimental group in the early months after treatment. For example, the treatment group in the drug court program could return to drug use following the program because they were no longer exposed to the treatment.
- Finally, outcome results could be affected by the *interaction of any of the preceding threats to internal validity.*

Variance The mean of the sum of all squared deviations from the mean of any distribution of scores.

Violence interrupters Within the context of the Operation CeaseFire program, the violence interrupters were expected to mediate conflicts before they escalated into shootings.

INDEX

A
Abstract or program summary, 128–129
  theory-driven, 129
  violence prevention model base, 129
Action setting, 4
Administrators
  experimental, 24
  program, 24–25, 28–29
  for program evaluation, 2–3, 18
  trapped, 24–25
Adult drug court programs logic model, 22–23, 23t
Allegiance, 4
American Evaluation Association, 26, 26t
Analysis. *See also* Meta-analysis; Scanning, analysis, response, assessment
  cost-benefit, 104f, 149
  cost-effectiveness, 149
  determining methods of, 21–22
  from focus group data, 42
Anti-crime programs, 142–143
Auto-regressive integrated moving average (ARIMA) model, 93, 135

B
Bar chart, 120, 120f
Before-and-after design, 91–93, 92t, 149–155
Benefits. *See also* Cost-benefit analysis
  diffusion of, 142, 150
  future costs and, 106–107
  reaping of, 107
Boundaries defined, 54–55

C
California Youth Authority (CYA), 87
Campbell, Donald T., 12, 24
Campbell Collaboration, 12, 149
CAPI. *See* Correctional Program Assessment Inventory
Causality, program impact theory and, 52
Causation question, 93–94
CBTs. *See* Cognitive-behavioral programs
Chi-test, 124–125
Classic experimental design, 80–85, 81t, 149
  advocates of, 86
  experimental groups in, 80–82, 150
  issues with, 86
  "Maryland Report" relating to, 85–87
  random control groups in, 80–82
  results of, 85–87
  threats to external validity, 84–85, 154
  threats to internal validity, 83–84, 154–155
  validity types in, 82–83
Client population, 131–133
Cognitive-behavioral programs (CBTs), 143–144
Communications, of evaluations, 136
Community forums, 40–43, 149
Community organization support, 134
Community policing program, 73–74
Comparison group, 88–89, 149
Conceptualization, 112–113, 149
Construct validity, 82, 149
Contract researcher, 29
Control groups, 88–89, 149
  random, 80–82
Conversational interview, 71–72
Correctional Program Assessment Inventory (CAPI), 50
Correctional Program Checklist (CPC), 75–76
Correlation, 125
Cost analysis
  of evaluation research, 143–144
  issues of, 99, 105
  in meta-analysis, 143
Cost-benefit analysis, 104f, 149
  and cost-effectiveness analysis, 107–108
  heart of, 103–104
Cost-effectiveness analysis, 149
  cost benefit analysis and, 107–108
  example of, 104–105
  heart of, 104–105
Cost-efficiency evaluation
  cost analyses limits, 108–109
  costs of, 99–108
  discussion questions for, 109–110
  introduction to, 97–99
  summary of, 109
Costs
  analyses of, 98–99
    assumptions and, 109
    importance of, 98–99
    issues with, 99, 105
    justification with, 99
    limits of, 108–109
  categories of, 100t
  of data collection, 21
  opportunity, 152
  projection of, 102

157

Costs, of cost-efficiency
        evaluation, 99-108
    cost analysis issues, 99, 105
    cost-benefit analysis heart,
        103-104
    cost-benefit and cost-
        effectiveness analysis,
        107-108
    cost-effectiveness analysis
        heart, 104-105
    examination of, 102
    future costs and benefits,
        106-107
    outcomes to, 103
    paying costs and reaping
        benefits, 107
    types of, 100-102
        direct *versus* indirect, 100
        hidden *versus* obvious, 101
        incremental *versus* sunk, 102
        opportunity, 101
        recurring *versus*
            nonrecurring, 100-101
        variable *versus* fixed, 101-102
    unit of analysis, 105-106
CPC. *See* Correctional Program
        Checklist
Crime and Justice Group. *See*
        Campbell Collaboration
Crime displacement, 142, 150
Criminal justice programs
    design of, 15-16, 47-48
    needs for, 31-32
    planning needs for, 33
Criminologists, 136
CYA. *See* California Youth
        Authority

D

D.A.R.E. *See* Drug Abuse
        Resistance Education
Data
    collection of
        costs of, 21
        for evaluation strategy,
            20-21
        for needs assessment
            evaluation, 37-38
        quality control of, 21

    strategies for, 20
    qualitative data, 34-35, 42
    quantitative data, 34-35, 42
Data analysis. *See* Measurement
        and data analysis
Data sources, for needs
        assessment evaluation,
        34-43
    current situation description,
        35-38
    current resources assessment,
        36
    data collection, 37-38
    population studied, 35-36
    social indicators, 36-37
    focus groups and community
        forums, 40-43
    analyze data, 42
    needs assessment and
        program planning, 42-43
    key informants, 39-40
    surveys, 38-39
    treatment groups, 39
Day reporting center (DRC),
        104-105
Decision making, 3
Descriptive statistics, 118-121
    bar chart, 120, 120*f*
    graphical displays, 119-121
    line graph, 121, 121*f*
    mean, 118
    median, 118
    mode, 118
    pie chart, 119-120
    standard deviation, 119
    variance, 119
Descriptive validity, 83, 150
Designs. *See specific designs*
Diffusion of benefits, 142, 150
Dimensions, 114
Direct *versus* indirect costs, 100
DRC. *See* Day reporting center
Drug Abuse Resistance Education
        (D.A.R.E.), 8, 55, 101

E

Effectiveness unit, 104
Efficiency. *See also* Cost-efficiency
        evaluation

    of evaluation measures
        development, 20
Empirical literature, 114
Ethical issues, of research, 25-29
Evaluability assessment approach,
        49-50, 150
    importance of, 49
    results of, 50
    steps for, 49-50
Evaluating logic and plausibility,
    of program theory, 59-60
Evaluation outcome. *See* Outcome
        evaluation
Evaluation research
    action setting, 4
    aim of, 5
    allegiance, 4
    call to action in
        best research design, 142
        conclusion to, 146
        cost analysis in, 143-144
        discussion questions for,
            146-147
        evidence-based practices, 144
        in field, 144-145
        future of, 146
        introduction to, 142
        practitioner partners, 145-146
        researchers involvement,
            142-143
    for decision making, 3
    demands for, 2
        public, 2
        service agencies, 2
        social problem, 2
    design of
        concerns about, 68
        monitoring conduct of, 66-68
        quality relating to, 66-67
        reassessing changes in, 67-68
    ethical issues of
        conducting research, 25-28
        social relationships in, 28-29
    judgmental quality, 3
    politics of, 24-25
    program-derived questions, 3
    publication, 4
    purpose of, 127-128
    role conflicts, 4

Evaluations. *See also* Impact evaluations; Needs assessment evaluation; Outcome evaluation; Process evaluation; Program evaluation; Reporting and using evaluations; Theory-driven evaluation
    designs of, 111–112
    development measures for, 19–20
        attitudinal, 20
        characteristics of, 20
        effectiveness, 19
        efficiency, 20
        impact factors of, 20
    forms of, 111–112
    indicators and, 113*t*
    issues with, 111–112
    literature about, 50–51
    process and impact, 137, 138*t*, 139
    researcher for, 28
    small-*n*, 86
    strategy for, 18–22
        analysis methods determination, 21–22
        data collection for, 20–21
        evaluation measures development, 19–20
        goal setting for, 18–19
        goal-objective relationship, 19
        S.M.A.R.T., 18–19
Evaluators. *See also* Principles, for evaluators
    beginning involvement of, 142–143
    participant as observer, 69–71
        concerns of, 70
        drawbacks to, 69
        fields notes of, 70–71
        guidelines for, 69–70
        objectivity of, 70
    for program evaluation, 2–3, 18, 25, 49
    with program implementation, 64–66

Evidence-based correctional program checklist, 75–76. *See also* Correctional Program Checklist
Evidence-based practices, 5–9, 144
    meta-analysis with, 144
Experimental administrator, 24
Experimental groups, 80–82, 150
Explicate program theory, 55
External validity, 82, 84–85, 150, 154

F
Focus groups, 150
    analyze data from, 42
    and community forums, 40–43, 149
    on community policing program, 73–74
    domination of, 75
    importance of, 41
    needs assessment and program planning with, 42–43
    observer and moderator with, 73
    for process evaluation, 73–75
    rationale for, 73
    relevance of, 41, 75
Funding, in process evaluation, 131

G
Gang Resistance Education and Training (GREAT), 48, 54–57
Goal-objective relationship, 19
Goals
    evaluation strategy setting of, 18–19
    for needs assessment evaluation, 42–43
    program, 55–56, 114
Gossett, W. S., 123
Graphical displays, 119–121
GREAT. *See* Gang Resistance Education and Training

H
Hidden *versus* obvious costs, 101
Host organization, 130–133, 150

Hot spots, 5–6, 135, 150
Hot-spot policing, 142

I
Impact evaluations
    presentation of, 135
    process and, 137, 138*t*, 139
Impact theory, 51–52, 150
Implicit program theory, 54
    define boundaries of, 54–55
    explicate program theory, 55
    program functions, components, activities defined, 56
    program goals and objectives defined, 55–56
    program theory description corroborated, 56–57
Incidence, 34
Incremental *versus* sunk costs, 102
Indicators, 113, 113*t*. *See also* Social indicators
Inferential statistics, 121–126
Internal validity, 82–84, 150, 154–155
Interval levels, 115–116
Interviewing, 150
    approaches to, 71–73
    definition of, 71
    principle of, 72–73
    for process evaluation, 71–73
Interviews
    conversational, 71–72
    open-ended, 72
Item construction, 112–115
    steps of, 112–113

J
Judgmental quality, 3

K
Key informants, 39–40, 150

L
Law Enforcement Assistance Administration (LEAA), 87
Line graph, 121, 121*f*

Literature
  empirical, 114
  evaluation, 50–51
Logic model, 22–23, 64–65, 150–151
  for adult drug court programs, 22–23, 23*t*
  elements of, 22
  explanation of, 22
  theory of, 22

M

Management by walking around (MBWA), 144–145
"Maryland Report", 6–9, 7*t*, 12–13, 151
  experiments relating to, 85–87
  what doesn't work?, 8
  what works?, 6–7
  what's promising?, 7–8
MBWA. *See* Management by walking around
Mean, 118, 151
Measurement and data analysis
  conceptualization with, 112–113, 149
  data with
    primary, 111–113
    secondary, 112–113
  dimensions relating to, 114
  discussion questions for, 126
  with empirical literature, 114
  indicators with, 113, 113*t*
  introduction to, 111–112
  measurement, 112–117
    item construction, 112–115
    levels of, 115–116
    validity and reliability, 116–117
    operational definitions relating to, 115–116, 151
  of program goals, 114
  of program inputs, resources, environment, 114
  of program processes, 114
  statistical tools, 117–126
    descriptive statistics, 118–121
    inferential statistics, 121–126
  summary of, 126

Measurement levels, 115–116
  interval, 115–116
  nominal, 115
  ordinal, 115
  ratio, 116
Media, 32
Median, 118, 151
Meta-analysis, 9–11, 151
  cost analysis included in, 143
  definition of, 9
  evidence-based practice with, 144
  example of, 10–11
  performance of, 9–10
  provisions of, 9
  research of, 10
Mode, 118, 151
Moderator, with focus groups, 73
Monitoring
  of evaluation research design, 66–68
  of process evaluation, 64
  of program evaluation, 3
  with program implementation, 64–66

N

Needs, 151
  definition of, 32–34
  estimation of, 34
  program duration for, 33–34
  resource distribution for, 33–34
Needs assessment evaluation
  data sources for, 34–43
  discrepancies with, 32–33
  discussion questions for, 44
  introduction to, 31–32
  outcome goals for, 42–43
  problems with, 43–44
  for program planning, 42–43
  steps in, 35*t*
  summary of, 44
Nominal levels, 115

O

Observer as participant, 151
One-group time-series design, 92–93, 92*t*, 151
Open-ended interview, 72

Operation CeaseFire Chicago review, 128–136, 151
  abstract or program summary, 128–129
  theory-driven, 129
  violence prevention model base, 129
  impact evaluation presentation, 135
  process evaluation presentation, 130–134
    client population in, 131–133
    community organization support for, 134
    confidentially with, 133
    funding in, 131
    host organization, 130–133
    outreach workers in, 131–133
    problems with, 132–134
    program evaluator for, 128, 130–134
    program headquarters, 130
    program management in, 131–133
    program operations in, 131
    sites and partners selection, 130
    staff in, 131–134
    target population in, 131–132
  supporting theory for, 129–130
    risk criteria in, 129
    risk management approach, 129
    target population in, 129
Operational definition, 115–116, 151
Opportunity costs, 101, 152
Ordinal levels, 115
Outcome evaluation, 152
  before-and-after design, 91–93, 92*t*, 149–155
  causation question, 93–94
  classic experimental design, 80–85, 81*t*, 149
  discussion questions for, 94
  to experiment or not to experiment, 85–87
  introduction to, 80
  purpose of, 80

quasi-experimental research design, 87–91, 89t, 152
summary of, 94
Outcome goals, for needs assessment evaluation, 42–43
Outreach workers in, 131–133

P

Pie chart, 119–120
Plausibility, of program theory, 59–60
POP. *See* Problem-oriented policing
Population
 client, 131–133
 study of, 35–36
 target, 129, 131–132
Practices
 evidence-based, 5–9
 and research comparison, 60–61
Practitioner partners, 145–146
Prevalence, 34
Primary data, 111–113
Principles, for evaluators, 26t, 28
 competence, 26
 integrity and honesty, 26–27
 respect for people, 27
 responsibilities, for general and public welfare, 28
 systematic inquiry, 26, 26t
Problem-oriented policing (POP), 16–18, 152
 concerns about, 17–18
 definition of, 17
 requirements for, 16–17
 research on, 17
Process and impact evaluations, 137, 138t, 139
Process evaluation, 152
 discussion questions for, 77
 evaluation research design conduct monitoring, 66–68
 evidence-based correctional program checklist, 75–76
 introduction to, 63–64
 monitoring of, 64
 program implementation, 64–66

qualitative methods used for, 69–75
 evaluator: participant as observer, 69–71
 focus groups, 73–75
 interviewing, 71–73
 summary of, 76–77
Process evaluation process. *See* Operation CeaseFire Chicago review
Program evaluation
 answers from, 24
 collaborative evaluation promoted by, 137
 planning of
  discussion questions for, 29–30
  evaluation research ethical issues, 25–29
  evaluation research politics, 24–25
  evaluation strategy, 18–22
  introduction to, 15–16
  logic model in, 22–23
  problem-oriented policing in, 16–18
  steps for, 18
  summary of, 29
 starting of
  administrator for, 2–3, 18
  Campbell Collaboration, 12, 149
  discussion questions for, 13
  effectiveness with, 1–2, 5
  evaluator for, 2–3, 18, 25, 49
  evidence-based practices with, 5–9
  introduction to, 1–2
  meta-analysis with, 9–11
  monitoring with, 3
  strengths and weaknesses of, 3–5
  summary of, 12–13
Program theory, 47–48, 152. *See also* Implicit program theory
 analyzing of, 57–61
  evaluating logic and plausibility of, 59–60

issues with, 59–60
 research and practice comparison, 60–61
 social needs linked to, 58–59
 articulation of, 48
 describing and producing of, 50–57
 perspectives of, 51
 scrutiny of, 48
Program-derived questions, 3
Programs. *See also* Adult drug court programs logic model; Correctional Program Assessment Inventory; Criminal justice programs; Explicate program theory; Implicit program theory
 administrators for, 24–25, 28–29
 anti-crime, 142–143
 CBTs, 143–144
 community policing, 73–74
 duration of, 33–34
 evaluators for, 128, 130–134
 goals for, 55–56, 114
 headquarters and, 130
 impact theory for, 51–52, 150
  causality and, 52
  stages of, 52
 implementation of, 64–66
  considerations of, 64
  evaluator with, 64–66
  issues with, 65
  logic model with, 64–65
  monitoring with, 64–66
  schedule for, 64–65
  scope of, 64
 inputs, resources, environment for, 114
 management for, 53, 131–133
 needs assessment evaluation for, 42–43
 operations for, 131
 organizational plan for, 51–57, 152
  elements of, 53
  program management and, 53
 processes for, 114

Propensity score matching (PSM), 90–91, 152
Public value, 143–144, 152
Publication, 4

Q
Qualitative data, 34–35, 42
Qualitative methods, for process evaluation, 69–75
  evaluator: participant as observer, 69–71
  focus groups, 73–75
  interviewing, 71–73
Quality control, of data collection, 21
Quantification, 112
Quantitative data, 34–35, 42
Quasi-experimental research design, 87–91, 89t, 152
  comparison groups in, 88–89, 149
  control groups in, 88–89, 149
  example of, 87–88
  PSM with, 90–91, 152
  recidivism found in, 88
  results of, 88
  self-drop group in, 89–90, 153
  treated and untreated groups in, 87–89

R
Random assignment, 80–81
Random control groups, 80–82
Rate of return, 107, 152
Ratio levels, 116
Recidivism, 88, 143
Recurring *versus* nonrecurring costs, 100–101
Regression, 126
Relationships. *See also* Social relationships, ethics and
  goal-objective, 19
Reliability, validity and, 116–117
Reporting and using evaluations
  discussion questions for, 139–140
  introduction to, 127–128

Operation CeaseFire Chicago review, 128–136
  abstract or program summary, 128–129
  host organization in, 130–133
  impact evaluation presentation, 135
  process evaluation presentation, 130–134
  supporting theory for, 129–130
  results of, 136–139
    communications relating to, 136
    criminologists and, 136
    influencing factors of, 137
    stakeholders and, 136–137
  summary of, 139
Representativeness, 38
Research. *See also* Evaluation research
  design of
    hot-spot policing relating to, 142
    methodological issues with, 142
    quality of, 142
  ethical issues with, 25–28
  of Meta-analysis, 10
  on POP, 17
  and practice comparison of program theory, 60–61
Resources
  assessment of, 36
  distribution of, 33–34
Results
  of classic experimental design, 85–87
  of evaluability assessment approach, 50
Risk criteria, 129
Risk management, 129
Role conflicts, 4

S
Scanning, analysis, response, assessment (SARA), 16, 152–153

Secondary data, 112–113
Self-drop group, 89–90, 153
Service agencies, 2
Service utilization plan, 51–53, 153
Sites and partners selection, 130
Skewness, 117
Small-n evaluations, 86
S.M.A.R.T. *See* Specific, measurable, attainable, relevant, time-bound
Social indicators, 36–37, 153
  issues with, 37
  role of, 36
  types of, 37
  uses of, 37
Social needs, program theory linked to, 58–59
Social problem, 2
Social relationships, ethics and, 28–29
  of contract researcher, 29
  of evaluation researcher, 28
  of program administrators and staff, 28–29
Specific, measurable, attainable, relevant, time-bound (S.M.A.R.T.), 18–19, 153
Stakeholders, 136–137
Standard deviation, 119, 153
Statistical conclusion validity, 82, 153
Statistical significance, 122–123
Statistical tools, 117–126
  chi-test, 124–125
  correlation, 125
  descriptive statistics, 118–121
  inferential statistics, 121–126
  logic of, 121–123
  regression, 126
  t-test, 123–124
Statistics, 112
Strategies. *See also* Evaluations
  for data collection, 20
Supporting theory, 129–130
Surveys, for needs assessment evaluation, 38–39
Systematic inquiry, 26, 26t
Systematic review, 5, 153. *See also* Maryland Report

T

Target population, 129, 131–132
Theory-driven evaluation
  analyzing of, 57–61
  articulation of, 48
  describing and producing of, 50–57
  discussion questions for, 61
  evaluability assessment approach to, 49–50
  introduction to, 47–49
  perspectives of, 51
  program impact theory, 51–52, 150
  program organizational plan, 51–57, 152
  program theory, 47–48, 152
  scrutiny of, 48
  service utilization plan, 51–53, 153
  summary of, 61

Theory-driven program, 129
Threats
  to external validity, 84–85, 154
  to internal validity, 83–84, 154–155
Tools. *See* Statistical tools
Trapped administrator, 24–25
Treated and untreated groups, 87–89
Treatment groups, for needs assessment evaluation, 39
t-Test, 123–124

U

Unit
  of analysis, 105–106
  of effectiveness, 104

V

Validity
  construct, 82, 149
  descriptive, 83, 150
  external, 82, 84–85, 150, 154
  internal, 82–84, 150, 154–155
  reliability and, 116–117
  statistical conclusion, 82, 153
  types of, 82–83
Value of life, 108–109
Variable *versus* fixed costs, 101–102
Variance, 119, 155
Violence interrupters, 133–134, 155
Violence prevention model base, 129

Y

YMCA leaders, 39–40, 42